Introduction

Agates are among the most fascinating and popular of the world's gemstones. Tens of millions of these nodules of natural silica occur in volcanic rock many millions of years old in various parts of the world. When cut open, agates can display an amazing wealth of colours and patterns of a beauty often surpassing the achievements of the human artist. No two agates are exactly alike, yet all are thought to have been formed by one natural process, albeit a process that remains, in part, a tantalizing mystery.

The popularity of agate has given rise since World War II to an absorbing and rewarding hobby, and clubs have been formed whose members collect and polish agates. In spite of this interest, no book adequately illustrated in colour has previously been produced about British agates, or indeed about the agates of any other country, although short articles in magazines are common. The purpose of this book, therefore, is to introduce these beautiful works of nature to people unaware of them, and to present the latest information on British agates.

The first section of the book defines and describes agates, outlines their distribution and occurrence in the British Isles, and presents a novel theory of agate formation based on old and new information. The central section deals, in detail, with representative agates from the British Isles, especially from Scotland which is rich in agates of unsurpassed beauty and variety. A detailed list of agate localities (which includes many national grid reference numbers) is also given. The final part of the book deals with collecting, cutting and polishing agates; agates around the world; followed by a glossary of the main terms and a bibliography.

Most of the agates illustrated are taken from the collections of the National Museums of Scotland, which probably possess the most extensive and select collection of agates in the British Isles as a result of the continuing interest in agates of former mineral curators, particularly Professor M. Forster Heddle, a legendary agate collector. Other agates illustrated are from the collections of the British Museum (Natural History) and the Geological Museum in London.

The author was fortunate to have been curator of the extensive mineral and gemstone collections of the National Museums of Scotland, Edinburgh, where the study of agates was one of his main interests.

Part and counterpart of halved agate (see also fig 54) and detail (*opposite*)

1 Broken agates in rock

3 Loose agates showing skins

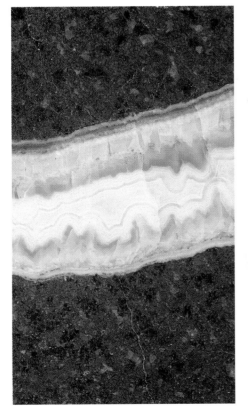

2 Volcanic rock showing vein agate (polished)

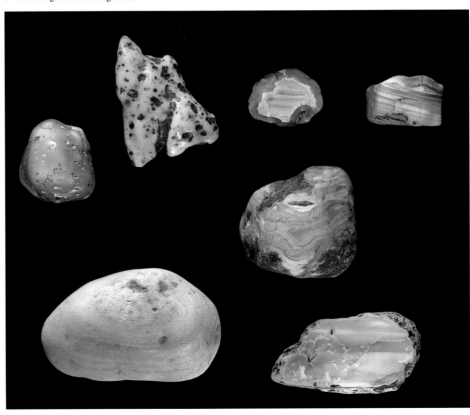

4 Typical beach agates

What are agates?

Agates are nodular masses, generally less than 15 cm in diameter, comprising one or more varieties of the common mineral quartz. Quartz consists essentially of the chemical elements silicon and oxygen, but exhibits many varieties of colour and form. Agates usually occupy the sites of former gas cavities (vesicles) in the volcanic rocks andesite and basalt (fig 5), or more rarely may be found filling open cracks or fissures in these rocks. This kind of agate is called vein agate (fig 2). Agates also occur in various other rocks, such as sediments. Agates characteristically display a greenish skin. Their interiors are strikingly different from their exteriors, as can be seen if a piece of agate-bearing rock is broken open (fig 1).

Agates can also be found as loose stones, set free from volcanic lavas when these soften and crumble through natural weathering. The agates are unaffected by weathering and remain hard and resistant, although their green skins may be abraded and eventually lost on being tumbled about, for example, by the action of the sea (figs 3 and 4). Abraded agates can look much like other pebbles on a beach and it is often difficult to distinguish them until one learns to recognize their characteristic features.

Some of these features can be seen when an agate is cut open with a special saw which consists of a power-driven disc of mild steel, with an outer rim impregnated with finely crushed diamonds. The agate is held in a vice, then pushed against the rotating diamond saw-blade (fig 129). Agates are commonly cut into halves (fig 6). Cutting agates reveals that they vary not only in the kinds but in the amounts of quartz present. They may consist entirely of *chalcedony* (a very fine grained variety of quartz), or of chalcedony in association with one or more of the following varieties; common quartz,

5 Whole agates enclosed in volcanic rock

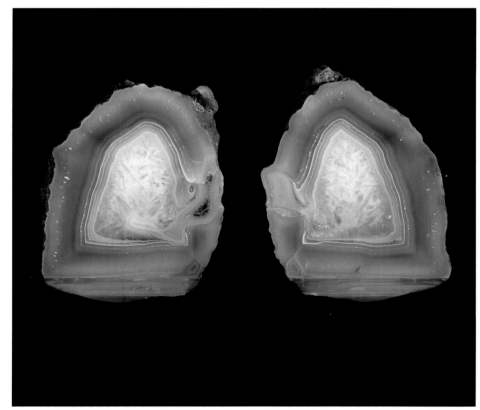

6 Polished halves of a cut agate

amethyst, smoky quartz, carnelian and jasper. Other minerals such as calcite (calcium carbonate) and celadonite (a green silicate mineral) are common associates of the aforementioned varieties of quartz. As it is prudent for anyone interested in collecting and studying agates to learn to recognize such mineral assemblages, a selection of cut and polished agates each showing more than one variety of quartz or more than one mineral is illustrated in figs 7 to 12. In nature there can be even more combinations than these.

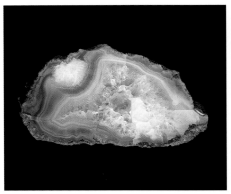

8 Agate composed of (central) purple amethyst enclosing cream-coloured calcite, surrounded by greyish chalcedony

10 Jasp agate (the orange-yellow portions are jasper)

12 *Opposite*: agate composed (from centre outwards) of calcite, brown (or smoky) quartz, ordinary quartz and grey-blue chalcedony

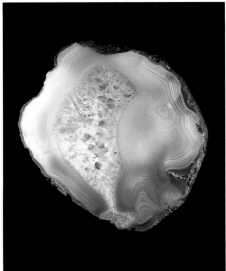

7 Agate composed of banded chalcedony and (central) quartz

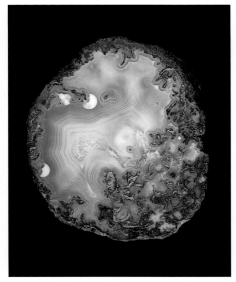

9 Agate with chalcedony enclosing curly wisps of green celadonite

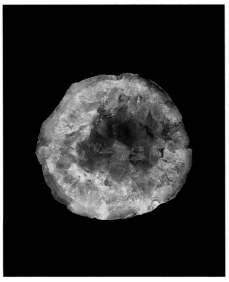

11 Carnelian agate (not polished)

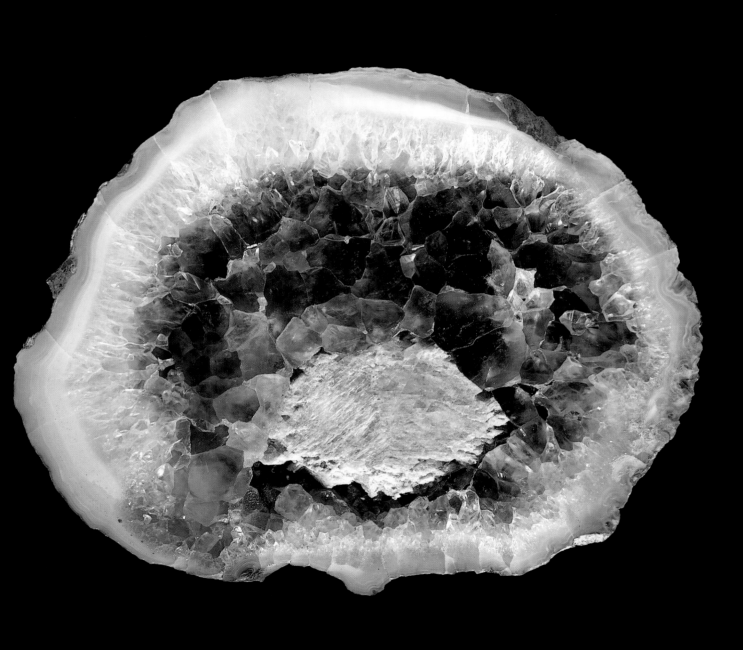

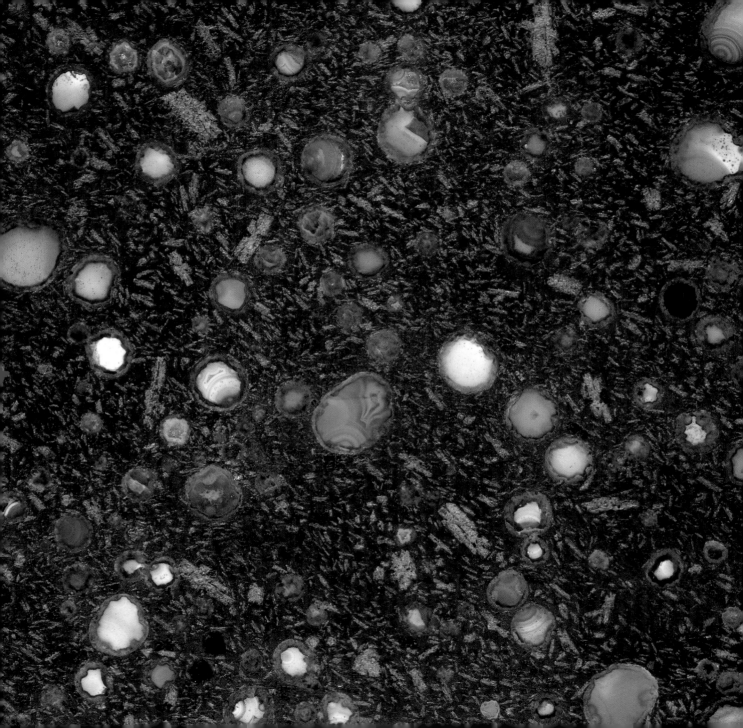

The agate-bearing rocks of the British Isles

The agates discussed in this book occur only within volcanic rocks. Such rocks are widely distributed within the British Isles, but agates do not occur in all of these. The map in fig 16 shows the distribution of volcanic rocks of four different geological ages. Of these, the Lower Palaeozoic lavas (about 470 million years old) and the Permo-Carboniferous lavas (about 320 million years old) are rarely agate-bearing. The Tertiary lavas (about 50 million years old) distributed in Northern Ireland and along the western seaboard of Scotland sometimes carry agates, for example in the islands of Rhum and Mull. The Old Red Sandstone lavas of Scotland (about 380 million years old) are the greatest treasure houses for agates. Most British agates are found in such rocks within the Midland Valley of Scotland (fig 17).

The rocks containing agates are frequently called *amygdaloids* (or amygdaloidal rocks). Such terms refer to lavas containing almond-shaped gas bubbles filled with secondary minerals (commonly light-coloured); these filled gas cavities are called *amygdales*. The secondary minerals include calcite, quartz, agate and chlorite. The shapes of the amygdales can vary greatly from the typical almond shape (figs 13 to 15) and are sometimes totally irregular.

The name Old Red Sandstone refers (in Scotland) to a thick sequence of reddish, non-marine, sedimentary rocks, chiefly sandstones, conglomerates and shales, and the agate-bearing lavas occur within these sandstones. These Old Red Sandstone volcanic rocks were laid down not as one great continuous pile of lava flows but as a number of thin (1 to 10 metre) lava flows which issued intermittently from scattered volcanic centres in the Midland Valley of Scotland, for example near Montrose and in the Ochil Hills. When volcanism ceased for a time the volcanic flows were weathered in part by natural elements, causing them to alter in composition and to break down into soft rock or even soil where vegetation grew and animals roamed. The volcanoes became active again and new lava flows covered the surfaces of the old flows. These processes occurred for millions of years until volcanism eventually ceased and the last of the lavas cooled down.

The formation of lava flows and the formation of agates are not contemporaneous or even connected events. Indeed, modern research has shown that agates do not form in the final cooling stages of volcanic rocks as has often been assumed. In general it appears that it is only after complete cooling and burial of the flows to a depth of 100 to 200 metres that silica-bearing solutions penetrate the lavas and fill some of the vesicles with agate-forming material. The formation of agates occurs over a range of low temperatures, perhaps averaging 100°C.

13 *Opposite*: an amygdaloid showing many enclosed agates (polished surface)

14 A vesicular lava showing empty gas cavities

15 A typical amygdaloidal lava

16 Distribution of volcanic rocks in the British
Isles

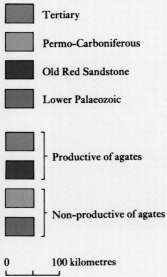

Key:

Tertiary

Permo–Carboniferous

Old Red Sandstone

Lower Palaeozoic

Productive of agates

Non-productive of agates

0   100 kilometres

Edinburgh

Belfast

Dublin

Cardiff

London

17 Distribution of Old Red Sandstone lavas in
the Midland Valley of Scotland

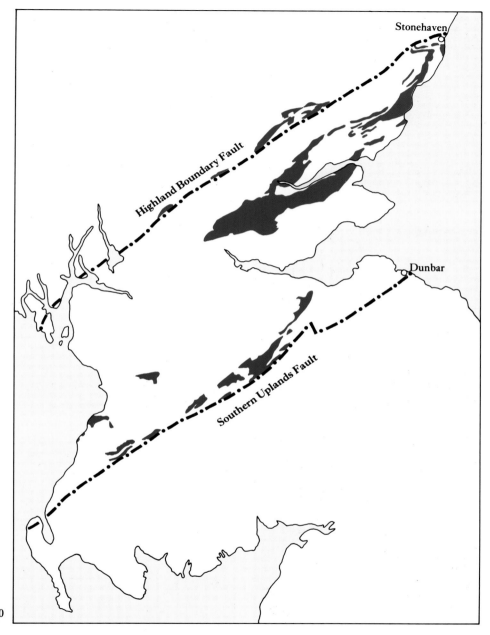

Stonehaven

Highland Boundary Fault

Dunbar

Southern Uplands Fault

Key:

Old Red Sandstone lavas

Major fault

0   50 kilometres   100

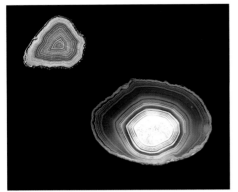

18 Layers in agates, one with quartz centre

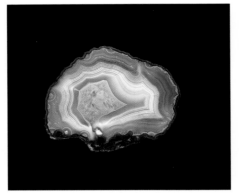

21 Skin within clear chalcedony layer

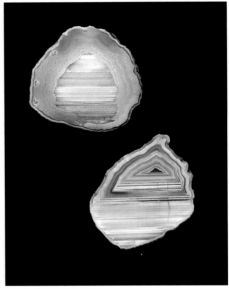

24 Onyx agates

19 Clear chalcedony layer in agates

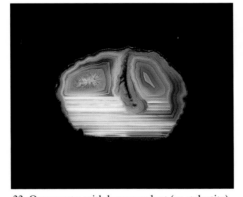

22 Onyx agate, with large pendant (or stalactite)

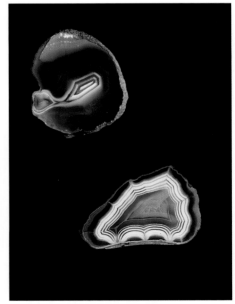

25 Tubes of escape, one with a large dilatation

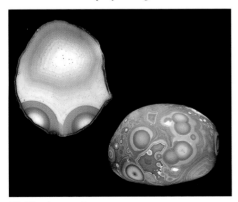

20 Hemi agates in agates

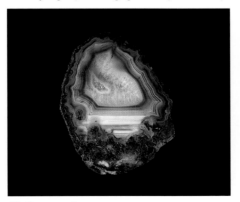

23 Onyx scenic agate

The mysterious formation of agates

In almost all cases there occurs on the tube of escape a dilatation of considerable size. This is situated near the point where the tube reaches the earliest-deposited layer of Chalcedony. It is filled somewhat posteriorly to the centre of the agate, but generally with the same material – Quartz.

No attempt has been made to explain this dilatation, although probably the whole secret of agate-formation is connected with its presence. It resembles the congestion which takes place when a moving stream of persons is arrested at a narrow exit.

M. Forster Heddle, *The Mineralogy of Scotland* (1901)

26 M. Forster Heddle, Professor of Chemistry, University of St Andrews (1862–84)

Agates have been collected and fashioned by man for thousands of years, yet until recently little was known about their origin and formation. During the last 200 years many investigators both professional and amateur have sought the secret of agate formation – but so far without complete success. The characteristic features of agates, though not difficult to recognize, are extremely difficult to explain and prove scientifically as they have not yet been investigated by currently available methods of experimental mineralogy.

These characteristic features were first described by M. F. Heddle in 1901 and are listed below, followed by a short account of past theories which have attempted to explain the formation of agates, together with the presentation of a novel theory.

Bands of chalcedony are usually clearly visible in cut or broken agates, while most agates possess a *centre of quartz* (fig 18).

Many agates show a narrow outermost band called the *clear chalcedony layer* (fig 19).

Some agates show *hemi agate,* sometimes called eye agate (fig 20).

Many agates have a green *skin,* wisps of which may protrude into the agate, especially into the clear chalcedony layer (fig 21).

A significant number of agates possess horizontal parallel layers of chalcedony, generally whitish in colour, called *onyx.* These onyx layers may terminate abruptly within the agate, but sometimes some of the layers will proceed from their terminations to follow around the contours of the upper part of the agate (figs 22 to 24).

Some agates possess a structure called a *tube of escape,* which is often associated with a balloon-shaped structure called a *dilatation on the tube of escape* (fig 25).

A feature commonly associated with tubes of escape (with or without dilatations) is a *rent* (or crack) in the clear chalcedony layer. This rent in turn is often seen to lead directly to a minute raised marking on the exterior of the agate here called an *agate dyke* (figs 27 and 28; see also fig 37).

In summary, the characteristic features of an agate are: skin; clear chalcedony layer; hemi agate; banded chalcedony; onyx bands; central quartz; tube of escape; dilatation on the tube of escape; rent; and agate dyke.

27 Tube of escape, rent and agate dyke

28 Tube of escape, rent and agate dyke (detail)

Most theories accounting for the formation of agates begin by explaining the formation of gas cavities in lavas. Molten lavas contain variable amounts of gas or steam and, as lavas cool after extrusion, this gas may escape quickly into the atmosphere. Sometimes, however, some of it becomes trapped near the tops of flows and held as bubbles within the lava as it continues to cool down, producing a cold lava that is full of small holes (vesicles). A source of silica such as a silica-bearing solution must then be present to penetrate and fill the vesicles. Views differ as to how the silica material gets into the cavities. It is at this point that the theories produce two main contradictory streams of thought.

One school of thought holds that dilute solutions of silica enter the cavities through all points in their walls and precipitate thin deposits of silica against them. This silica precipitate later crystallizes as chalcedony (a crystalline variety of quartz). An agate is thus built up gradually, and probably fitfully, by the continual ingress of silica-charged solutions followed by the exit of the same solutions when spent of their precipitate. This view can be called the 'In and Out' theory of agate formation.

A second school of thought, however, cannot accept that spent solutions can escape from cavities once the early formed layers have coated their inner walls and crystallized solidly against them. They suggest instead that dense silica gels are formed and remain inside the cavities. In the presence of unique factors operating within the containment of each cavity space, these gels undergo reconstitution whereby various chemical phases are segregated by diffusion, and eventually crystallize as systematic growth bands of chalcedony or quartz, or both. This view is more recent than the first and can be called the 'In and Sort Out' theory.

There are many variations of each of the above main theories but none have proved to be wholly acceptable. The most important classical theory, using internal rhythms, was proposed by R. E. Liesegang who suggested, early this century, that rhythmic precipitations of iron pigments spontaneously produce banded structures (Liesegang rings) in silica gels in rocks. The pigments are supposed to hinder or prevent subsequent crystallization of the gel so that the silica of agates also receives a banded morphology. Landmesser (1984), however, points out that these ideas of Liesegang are fully disproved by theoretical arguments as well as by microscopic investigations of the morphology of agates. There are definite morphologic differences between ordinary agate banding and Liesegang rings. The distribution of pigments in agates does not correspond to the laws of Liesegang rings. Furthermore the correlation between the distribution of pigments and the ordinary banding, as postulated by Liesegang, is not found in agates. Readers who are interested in a detailed history and evaluation of past theories should read Michael Landmesser's excellent article 'Das Problem der Achatgenese' (1984).

Careful consideration of all the available evidence gives rise to a third, new theory. It should be emphasized that this theory, like the others, is based to some extent on speculation as there are aspects of the process that remain a mystery. These aspects relate to the physical and chemical behaviour of dense silica gels under containment (as, for example, in vesicles), proven evidence of which will only be forthcoming when sophisticated methods of experimental mineralogy are applied to the study of such gels. This theory, which explains the genesis of the characteristic features of agate, is presented in diagrammatic form in figs 29 to 37. It is a version of the 'In and Sort Out' theory.

The theory begins with an empty gas cavity which, for convenience, shall be taken to be spherical, so yielding a central cross-section which is circular in outline (fig 29). The cavity is usually first lined with a green mineral skin which consists of one or more silicate minerals such as celadonite, chlorite and saponite. This skin is formed as a result of the movement of *meteoric waters* (that is, mainly water that has percolated downwards into rocks) through lava where it decomposes some of the constituent minerals and carries away from them certain chemical elements in solution. Some of these leached substances are deposited in gas cavities where they crystallize as a green mineral skin, effectively priming the walls of the vesicles (fig 30).

The vesicle is next penetrated by silica-bearing colloidal solutions which fill the vesicle wholly or partly with a dense silica gel. The origin of these solutions is as yet unknown: they do not seem to be an end-product of volcanism in which watery solutions typically occur, but are thought to be meteoric waters. Such waters leach constituents (including silica) from rock-forming minerals, and eventually deposit them in some of the empty vesicles as a very dense plastic-like gel (fig 31). In some agates the skin gets ruptured during this stage and fragments of it may hang down into the gel. This gel, composed mainly of silica with some water and impurities, is now contained in its own unique space. It is destined to increase even more in density until it reaches a crystalline state, a process beginning with the separation or segregation of its constituents into layers through a process of chemical differentiation and diffusion. It is these different layers which will crystallize as varieties of quartz. Each layer has its own composition of silica, water (sometimes there is none) and impurities such as pigmenting iron compounds (fig 32).

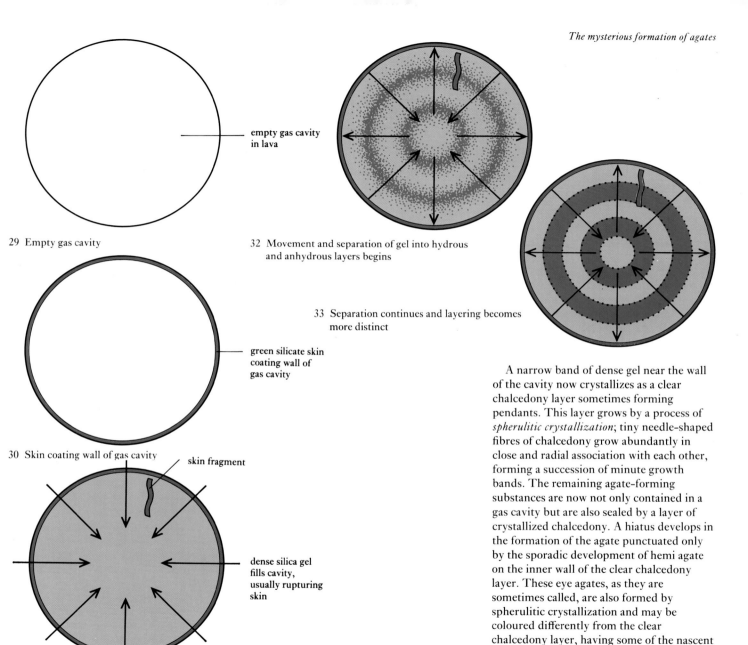

29 Empty gas cavity

empty gas cavity
in lava

30 Skin coating wall of gas cavity

green silicate skin
coating wall of
gas cavity

31 Dense silica gel fills cavity

skin fragment

dense silica gel
fills cavity,
usually rupturing
skin

32 Movement and separation of gel into hydrous
and anhydrous layers begins

33 Separation continues and layering becomes
more distinct

A narrow band of dense gel near the wall of the cavity now crystallizes as a clear chalcedony layer sometimes forming pendants. This layer grows by a process of *spherulitic crystallization*; tiny needle-shaped fibres of chalcedony grow abundantly in close and radial association with each other, forming a succession of minute growth bands. The remaining agate-forming substances are now not only contained in a gas cavity but are also sealed by a layer of crystallized chalcedony. A hiatus develops in the formation of the agate punctuated only by the sporadic development of hemi agate on the inner wall of the clear chalcedony layer. These eye agates, as they are sometimes called, are also formed by spherulitic crystallization and may be coloured differently from the clear chalcedony layer, having some of the nascent agate's impurities enclosed within them during their growth (figs 34 and 35).

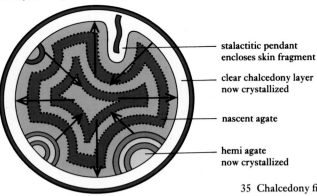

34 Clear chalcedony layer now crystallized

stalactitic pendant encloses skin fragment

clear chalcedony layer now crystallized

nascent agate

hemi agate now crystallized

long fibrous chalcedony

spherulitic crystallization of clear chalcedony layer

35 Chalcedony fibres in clear chalcedony layer
(spherulitic crystallization)

The segregated hydrous and anhydrous silica bands enclosed by the solid clear chalcedony layer may now progress to crystallization without the bands being distorted from a natural configuration within the vesicle, or the bands may be affected by dynamic forces arising within the vesicle. The nature of these forces is as yet unkown; they may be associated with shrinkage, expansion, initial crystallization growth, differences in super-saturation levels or other factors. Though the precise nature of these forces cannot be specified, we should not be deterred from recognizing that such forces must exist. The evidence lies in the obvious distortion of visible bands in some agates (figs 25, 27 and 28). In general, agates whose bands are distorted by forces prior to their crystallization will show marked irregularity in the course of their banding, with the possible formation of tubes of escape and dilatations (fig 36).

In some agates the dynamic forces are so intense that they cannot be relieved simply be creating tubes of escape and dilatations. Only when the clear chalcedony layer is actually torn by pressure from the tubes and/or dilatations is relief obtained. When this happens, a small amount of silica gel is

chalcedony layers now crystallized

quartz

dynamic flow lines of chalcedony layers

dilatation

agate dyke

rent in clear chalcedony layer

quartz

tube of escape

36 Tube of escape with dilatation,
rent in clear chalcedony layer, and
quartz within crystallized layers of chalcedony

expelled through the rent giving rise to the minutely raised features here called agate dykes (fig 37). Thus, depending on the nature of the containment forces, some nascent agates may show deformed banding.

Every agate is unique even though the rock environment is the same as regards pressure, temperature, and meteoric water compositions. Agates of totally different kinds and colours can grow side by side, each in its own unique and idiosyncratic abode. Only when the silica bands have evolved to a state of near crystallization does crystallization proper begin. Fibrous

chalcedony mixed with some fine granular quartz crystallizes as tiny growth bands, extending from the clear chalcedony layer towards the centre of the agate, and as it does so it divides the agate into sector zones. These growth bands and sector zones can be seen clearly under a microscope (figs 38, 39 and 40).

The above description of agate formation has omitted, in the interest of clarity and simplicity, an explanation of the formation of onyx (fig 41). Onyx bands appear to be due to the gravitational settling of large colloidal silica particles in a gel. On crystallizing, these form chalcedonic bands, often with much mixed granular quartz, and may be early or late in formation after the clear chalcedony layer has formed. Onyx agates will be further referred to in the chapter entitled 'A portfolio of British agates'.

Colour banding is commonly seen in agates but it is not the same as the systematic growth banding discussed above. Coloured bands in agate, despite their often striking appearance, are due to chance variations in pigment distribution. The pigments, the commonest of which are iron compounds, such as iron oxide, come mainly from the impurities mentioned above. Colour bands are also much broader than growth bands, and such broad bands do not mark separate growth stages or layers of crystallization within agates.

38 Growth layers and sector zones in concentric agate

39 Spherulitic crystallization in agate

40 Growth layers, sector zones and tube of escape in onyx agate

37 Relation of tube of escape and dilatation to rent and agate dyke (details of agate omitted)

41 Onyx agate (also showing fortification banding)

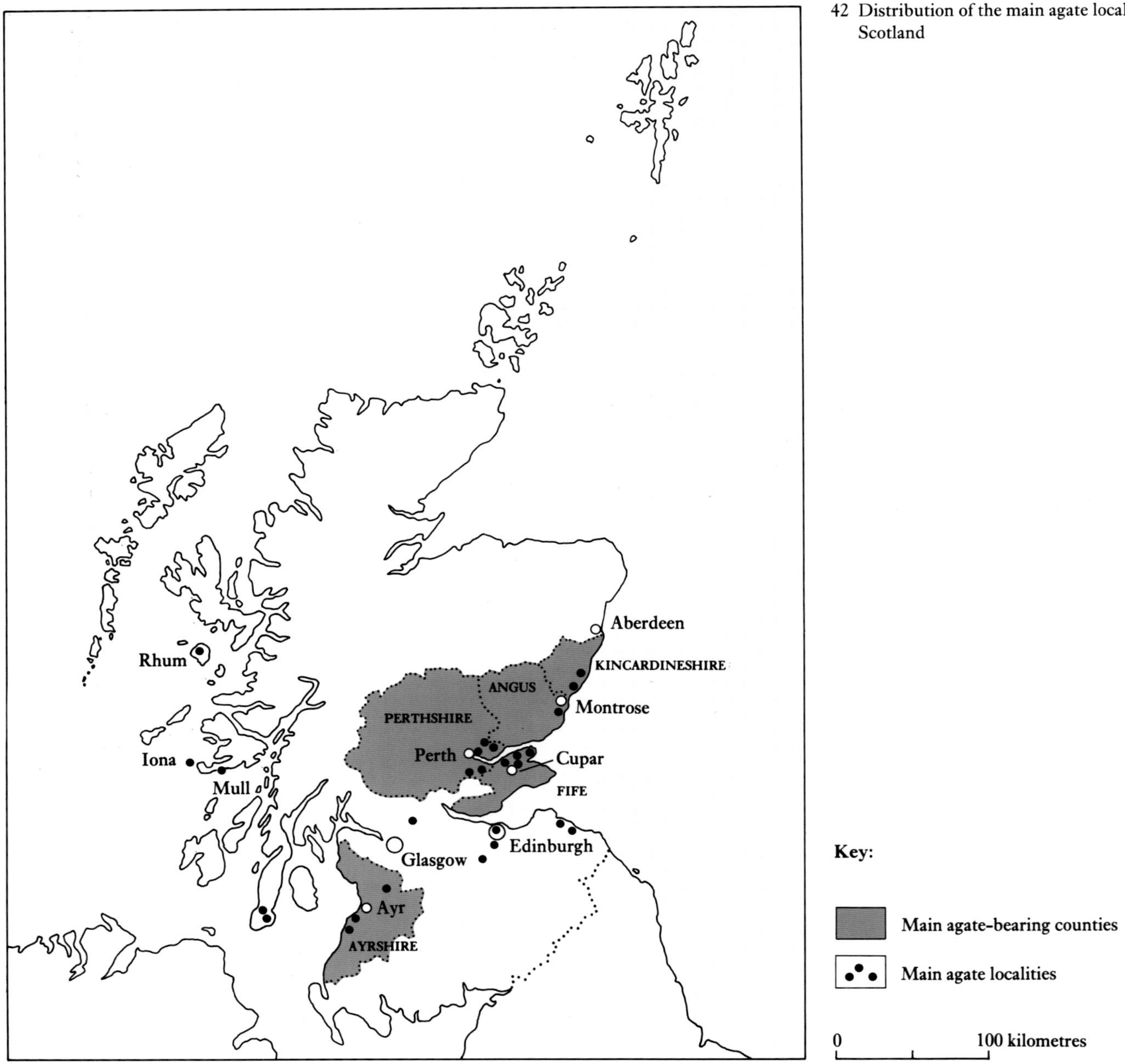

42 Distribution of the main agate localities in Scotland

British agate localities

The best quality agates are found in the Scottish counties of Kincardine, Angus, Fife and Ayrshire. Here they are found *in situ* in the Old Red Sandstone lavas, or loose on beaches and in riverbeds and fields. In England, Wales and Northern Ireland, agates are found mainly as loose specimens on beaches, while *in situ* localities are rare (figs 42 and 50). The names of selected agate localities in the British Isles are given below, together with (for Scotland) their national grid reference numbers which indicate the localities on both 1:50 000 and One-Inch Ordnance Survey maps. The locality name and national grid reference number here refer to areas of about a few hundred square metres. Thus a certain amount of searching will be necessary and advice on how to search is given in the chapter entitled 'Collecting agates'.

Most of the agate localities are accessible and situated in areas of scenic beauty where agates may be found on beaches, hills, cliffs and in streams (figs 43 to 49).

In the locality list below the data (for Scotland) are listed in the following order: locality name, grid reference number, map number of 1:50 000 series, and map number (in brackets) of One-Inch series: for example, Barras quarry NO 822790, 45, (43). National grid reference numbers in four figures imply less precision in defining a locality, generally because of its large size. Because most Scottish agate literature refers to county localities counties are referred to here, although they have been replaced by regions and districts.

Scottish agate localities
(taken mainly from M. F. Heddle's
The Mineralogy of Scotland (1901))

Kincardine
Barras quarry, NO 822790, 45 (43)
Allardice, NO 82 74, 45 (43)
Pulpit Rock, Kinneff, NO 850738, 45 (43)
Finella Den, NO 77 68, 45 (43)
St Cyrus, NO 75 65, 45 (43)

Angus
Ferryden, NO 725568, 54 (43, 50)
Scurdie Ness, NO 734568, 54 (43, 50)
Blue Hole, Usan, NO 72 55, 54 (43, 50)
Rock of St Skae, NO 715538, 54 (43, 50)
Lunan Bay railway cutting, NO 67 50, 54 (43, 50)
Near Ethie House, NO 69 47, 54 (50)
Panmure Den, NO 54 38, 54 (50)
East Balgay, NO 38 31, 54 (50)

Perth
Gourdie, NO 12 42, 53 (49)
Black Hill, NO 22 32, 53 (49)
Agate Knowe, Tinkletop, Ballindean and Inchture, NO 26 30, 53 (56, 49)
Pitroddie Den, NO 21 25, 58 (55)
Kinnoull Hill, NO 135226, 58 (55)
Near Pitkeathly, NO 11 17, 58 (55)
Path of Condie, NO 07 12, 58 (55)
Rossie Ochil, NO 09 13, 58 (55)
Binn Hill, Glen Farg, NO 17 14, 58 (49)

Fife
Norman's Law, NO 305198, 59 (56)
Balmeadowside, NO 318183, 59 (56)
Dunbog, NO 280180, 59 (56)
Carphin, NO 319195, 59 (56)
Luthrie, NO 335195, 59 (56)
Middlefield, NO 382155, 59 (56)
Balmerino, NO 36 25, 59 (56)
Scurr Hill, NO 367252, 59 (56)
Many other localities have been reported since Heddle's day from the land triangle apexed by the towns of Tayport, Cupar and Newburgh, including the shores of the Tay.

Ayr
Burn Anne, NS 522350, 70 (67)
South of the Heads of Ayr, NS 28 18, 70 (72)
Dunure, NS 25 16, 70 (72)
Agates occur at sites south of Dunure; at Culzean Castle and Maidens for example.

Shetland Islands
Northmaven, opposite Dore Holm, HU 22 77, 3 (2)

Inverness
Rhum, Bloodstone Hill beaches, NG 00 31, 39 (33)
Luinga Bheag island, non-volcanic, NM 62 87, 40 (34)

Stirling
Campsie Hills, very rarely in Carboniferous lavas, 64 (60)

Argyll
Iona, on the beaches, NM 27 24, 48 (51)
Ross of Mull, NM 45 19, 48 (51)
Machrihanish Bay, Kintyre, NR 63 21, 68 (65)
Killellan Hill, Kintyre, NR 68 16, 68 (65)

Midlothian
Blackford Hill, Edinburgh, vein agate, NT 255705, 66 (62)
Hillend, Pentland Hills, NT 252666, 66 (62)

East Lothian
Dunbar, NT 68 79, 67 (63)
Dunglass, on beach, NT 77 73, 67 (63)

Peebles
Carlops, vein agate, NT 16 56, 72 (62)
Linhouse, NT 06 62, 65 (61)

43 Usan House and Scurdie Ness, Angus

45 Ballindean, Perthshire

44 Kinnoull Hill, Perthshire

46 St Columba's Bay, Isle of Iona

47 Norman's Law in Fife

49 Agate-bearing field, northern Cheviot Hills (near Mindrum)

48 Burn Anne in Ayrshire

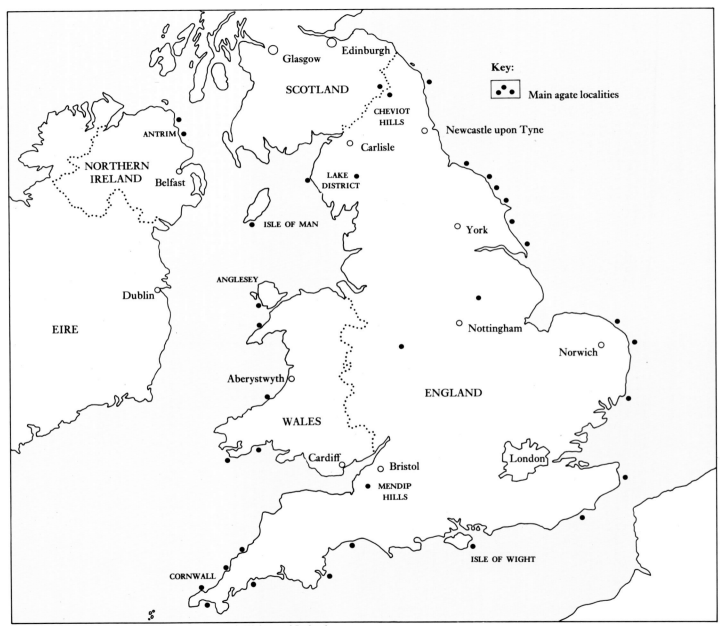

Key:

Main agate localities

SCOTLAND

Glasgow

Edinburgh

CHEVIOT HILLS

Newcastle upon Tyne

Carlisle

NORTHERN IRELAND

ANTRIM

Belfast

LAKE DISTRICT

EIRE

Dublin

ISLE OF MAN

ANGLESEY

York

Nottingham

Norwich

ENGLAND

Aberystwyth

WALES

London

Cardiff

Bristol

MENDIP HILLS

CORNWALL

ISLE OF WIGHT

50 Distribution of some agate localities in England, Wales, and Ireland

22

Agate localities in England, Wales, Northern Ireland and Eire

A search through the available publications of the various Geological Surveys revealed only a few mentions of agate localities. Even Greg and Lettsom's *Manual of the mineralogy of Great Britain and Ireland* (1858) lists agate for England only in Cornwall, Cumberland, Gloucestershire and Staffordshire.

England

The English localities are listed by county from north to south. These localities (and those for Wales and Ireland) are not well enough documented to enable National Grid References to be given.

Northumberland
Cheviot Hills, widely distributed. Found in streambeds or in farm fields. Beaches near Amble.

Cumberland
Carrock Fells
Falcon Craig, in Ordovician volcanic rocks
Fleswick Bay, Whitehaven, in beach shingle.

Yorkshire
Beaches along coast; for example, 3 kilometres south of Scarborough, and about 2 kilometres south of Robin Hood's Bay.

Derbyshire
In Carboniferous lavas near Buxton.
In chert rocks near Bakewell.

Nottinghamshire and Staffordshire
In glacial pebble deposits alongside the course of the River Trent.
In gravel near Lichfield, Staffordshire.

South coast of England, rarely
Kent beaches.
Sandown, Isle of Wight.

Somerset
Potato-stones from non-volcanic rock in the Mendip Hills.

Cornwall, poor-quality vein agate
Beach at Marazion.
Looe Bar, near Porthlevan.

Wales

Welsh agates are rare, and of moderate to poor quality in general.

Coastal areas near Aberystwyth
Some coastal sites in South Pembrokeshire and Mid-Glamorgan.
Some beaches on north side of Lleyn Peninsula.
In Ordovician basalts near Builth Wells, Powys.

Northern Ireland

North coast of Antrim, rarely.
Shores of Lough Neagh, reported in Greg and Lettsom (1858).

Eire

No reported occurrences of agate have been found.

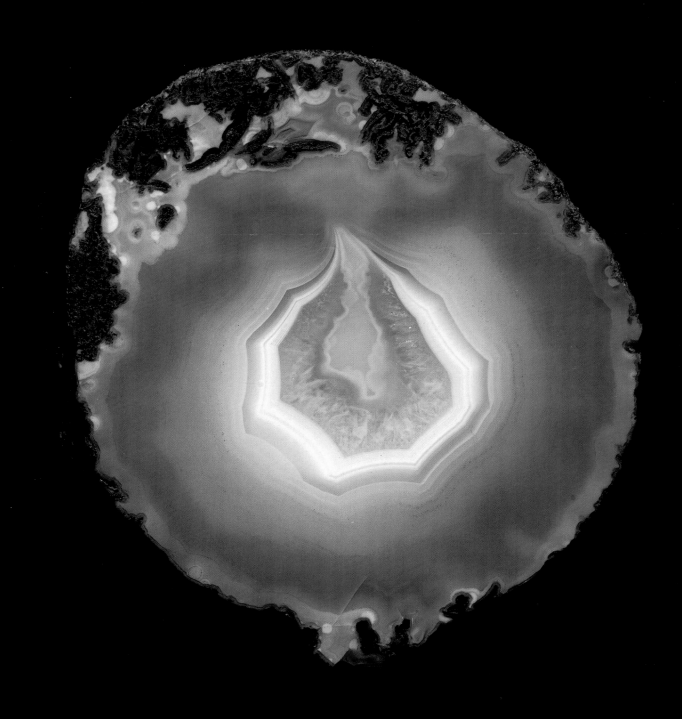

A portfolio of British agates

Agates from selected British localities are now illustrated, beginning with Scottish agates.

The agates from Scotland are described in a north to south geographical order using the following towns as agate-centres: Montrose, Perth, Cupar and Ayr. Agates from the islands of Mull, Iona and Rhum are also described (see fig 42).

The Montrose area

This area covers part of the former counties of Kincardine and Angus (now classified as parts of the regions of Tayside and Grampian). The Royal Burgh of Montrose is a well-known sailing, holiday and fishing port, with a long and interesting history.

The Blue Hole, Usan

This is, or was, the most famous agate locality in the British Isles. It was discovered in the nineteenth century but was exploited by only two or three collectors who extracted the best agates. The locality, some 3 kilometres south of Montrose and close to Usan House, is now covered over and lost to collectors. Fortunately, these agates were donated to the National Museums of Scotland by the original collectors Robert Miln, a wealthy business man (fig 53) and Matthew Forster Heddle, Professor of Chemistry at St Andrews University.

The most characteristic colours of these agates are brilliant inky-blue and white, but some yellow and red-brown are not uncommon. Sizes often ranged up to about 12 cm in diameter. The agates are of many types, and a selection is illustrated in figs 54 to 58.

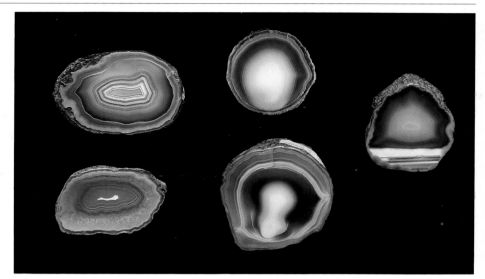

52 Blue Hole agates

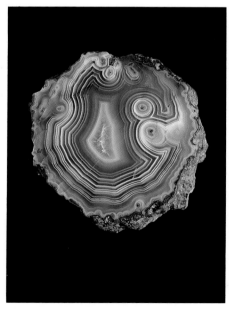

51 *Opposite*: Blue Hole agate (see also fig 57)

53 Robert Miln of Woodhill, Angus

54 Stalactitic and fortification Blue Hole agate

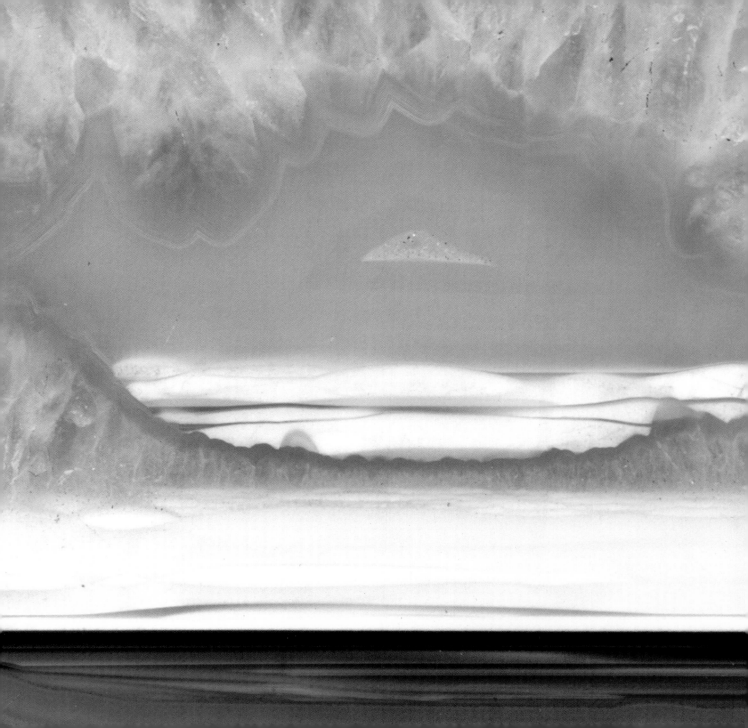

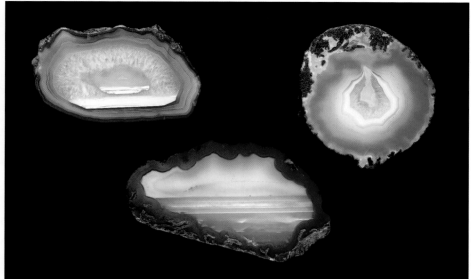

56 Blue Hole agates

57 Blue Hole agates

55 *Opposite*: detail from fig 57

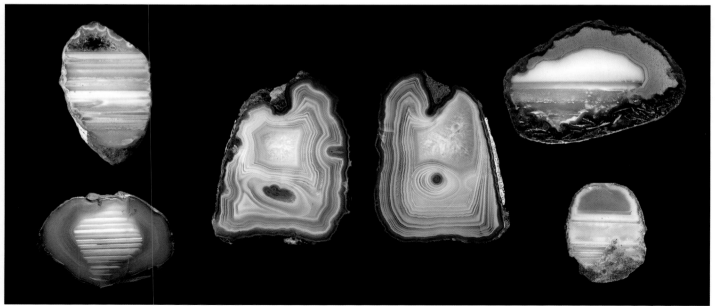

58 Blue Hole onyx agates

Scurdie Ness

Scurdie Ness is a promontory on the south side of the entrance to Montrose harbour. The beaches here, from Ferryden village (west of Scurdie Ness) to Boddin Point (south of Scurdie Ness), have long been favourite places for the agate hunter. Thus D. H. Edwards in his book *Among the Fisher Folk of Usan and Ferryden* (1921) recounts a fascinating tale about the 'Pebble Hoose':

> We have on many occasions engaged in the work of 'hauking' pebbles from the rocks at Usan, and have several specially finely marked specimens. Many of the visitors have been very lucky hunters, and possess well-polished stones set in brooches, pendants, sleeve-links, and ear-rings. The salmon fishers also secure not a few, one of these men having a complete outfit for cutting and polishing the stones in a snug little workshop attached to his bothy at Marywell, quite close to the ancient graveyard on the site where stood the chapel of St. Mary. That the work was engaged in with success about one hundred years ago is proved by the ruins of the cottage we have already spoken of as still to be seen 'along the braes', known as 'the pebble hoose'. In this humble and lonely abode, almost washed by the sea, a man lived by himself and worked as a lapidary. We believe specimens of his handicraft are to be seen in several mansions in the district – notably in Usan House, the top of a round table formed with stones of many colours, and set with fine taste and skill.

Scurdie agates (figs 59 to 65) are frequently pink or rich brown with colourless bands. Straight banded agates (onyx) are not common.

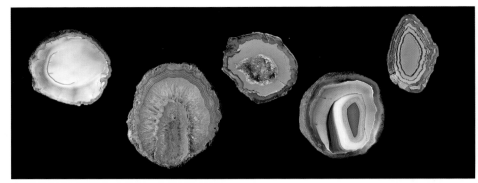

59 Agates from Scurdie Ness

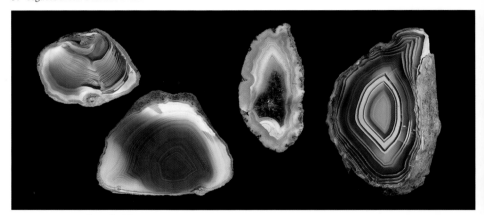

60 Agates from Scurdie Ness

61 Flame agate from Scurdie Ness

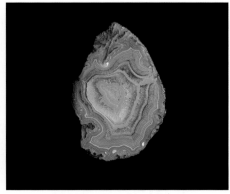

62 Complex fortification agate from Scurdie Ness

63 *Opposite*: detail from fig 62

65 Eye agate from Scurdie Ness

64 Onyx agate from Scurdie Ness (detail)

66 Onyx agate in matrix from St Cyrus

St Cyrus

St Cyrus village lies on the coast some 8 kilometres north of Montrose. A nature reserve with rich and unusual plant life covers 92 hectares round the village, and breeding seals and eider ducks visit the bay. Fine rock scenery can be enjoyed north-east of the village and its sandy beach. Agates of fine colours were exposed in the old railway cuttings to the north and south of St Cyrus. Onyx and eye agates in blue and white have been reported (fig 66).

The late Harry Scott of Edinburgh searched for and collected St Cyrus agates for more than twenty years. Some of these he collected below high vertical cliff faces, although he frequently warned young collectors about the obvious dangers inherent in such a practice. Sadly, whilst on a collecting trip in an area where he had discovered large agates of superb quality, the dangers became all too apparent as while hammering at and below a vertical cliff face, he loosened two or three tons of rock which fell on him, killing him instantly.

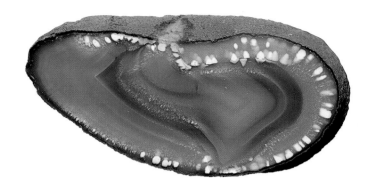

68 Deformation banding in Barras agate; agate dyke traverses the creamy-yellow patch as a fine line

67 Deformation banding in Barras agate

Barras Quarry

This quarry (more properly called Cotbank Quarry), opened in the late 1960s, has produced some fine agates, of which the host rock is a red-brown amygdaloid. Many collectors and clubs have visited this locality, particularly members of the Stanley and District Lapidary, Mineralogical and Geological Society, County Durham. One of this society's members collected a spherical agate some 25 cm in diameter, subsequently called 'big daddy'. Unfortunately, when cut open at the National Museums of Scotland, a large proportion of the agate was found to consist of quartz.

The most interesting of the Barras agates are the grey-blue ones displaying flow bands associated with white segregation spots, in which, where tubes of escape reach the outer wall, fine raised linear markings (referred to here as agate dykes) are found on the skin of the agate. These agates had suffered plastic deformation of their segregated layers (of the kind described on page 16) before final crystallization took place (figs 67 and 68).

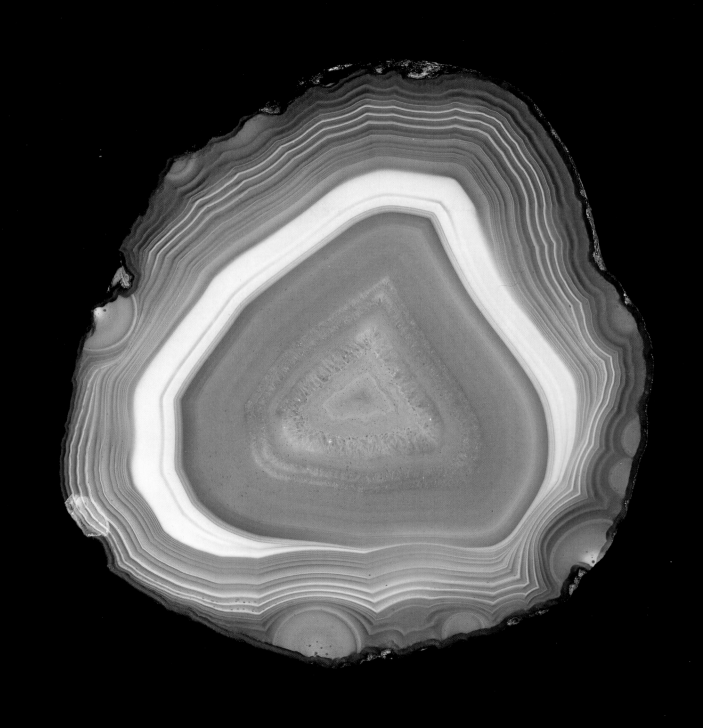

The Perth area

The agate-bearing rocks around the town of Perth lie in the former county of Perth which is now part of the Tayside Region. The Sidlaw Hills to the north-east and the Ochil Hills to the south-east of Perth both contain agate-bearing rocks.

Kinnoull Hill

This hill, immediately to the east of Perth, is over 220 metres high and on its southern side presents a frontage of rugged andesite rocks. Agates were formerly found in some abundance in the rocks at the foot of Kinnoull Hill. A selection of Kinnoull agates is shown here. The strongly marked red-brown-white agate (fig 69) clearly shows the skin, the clear chalcedony layer, reddish hemi agates, grey-white chalcedony layers, and a pinkish centre composed of alternating layers of chalcedony and quartz. The large elongate agate (fig 70), purchased over 100 years ago, is of interest mainly because of the legend inscribed on the reverse: 'Kinnoull Pebble, 5/6d' (28p). The other two cut agates were collected as recently as 1977. Another agate from Kinnoull, nicknamed 'rubber lips', is shown in fig 71.

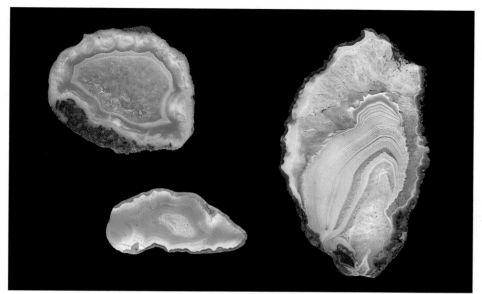

70 Kinnoull Hill agates

Ballindean

The name Ballindean is used here to cover a number of localities huddled together about 3 kilometres north-west of Inchture, a village some 22 kilometres east of Perth. These localities are: Agate Knowe, Ballindean Farm, Tinkletop, and Inchture itself. The agates found here have been described by M. F. Heddle (1901) as 'of the most delicate tints of lilac, flesh-red, and rose, in grey-blue chalcedony, often with an outer milk-white layer; the most exquisite and delicately-tinted agates known'. Ballindean agates include round-banded, fortification and stalactitic types (fig 72). Excellent tubes of escape are seen on two of the agates, while the clear chalcedony layer is prominent on many of the specimens. Quartz is only prominent in two of the agates.

69 *Opposite*: Kinnoull Hill agate

71 Kinnoull Hill agate

72 Agates from Ballindean

73 *Opposite*: detail of agate from Ballindean

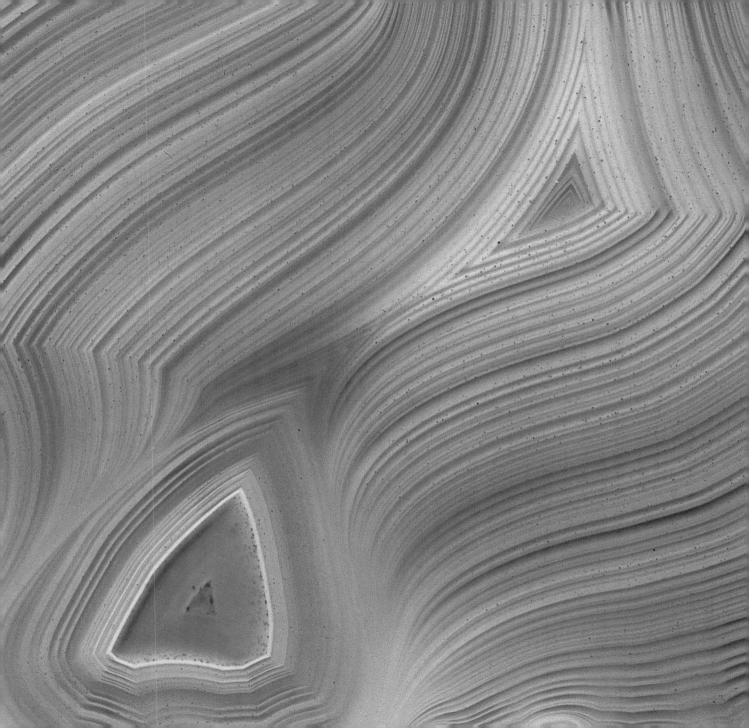

Black Hill

The Black Hill lies some 8 kilometres west-north-west of Ballindean. Substantial amounts of large agates (up to 15 cm for example) were discovered here during the mid-1960s (figs 74 and 75). The rectangular agate slice shows the clear chalcedony layer with a small pendant attached; red-brown, needle-shaped zeolite crystals, coated thickly by a clear chalcedony layer and forming much of the bottom right-hand half of the agate; and colourless quartz crystals enveloping the irregular 'central' part of the agate which is composed of pinky chalcedony layers. A few strands of green skin that originally fell into the nascent agate can also be seen. Large (35 to 40 cm) geodes (that is cavities lined by chalcedony and filled by quartz crystals pointing towards the centre of the cavity) have been found rarely in some parts of the Black Hill.

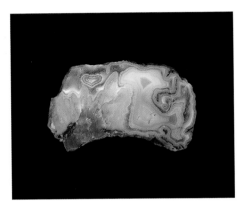

75 Zeolitic agate from Black Hill

76 Complex agate from Path of Condie

74 Agate from Black Hill

Path of Condie

This locality lies about 11 kilometres south-south-west of Perth and is only a few kilometres from the motorway to the east, but has a remote, even melancholy air. It has long been a popular collecting locality where fine and generously sized agates (10 to 12 cm, for example) have been found. Red-white and grey-white colours predominate in agates mainly of the fortification type. Some of these agates show fine examples of tubes of escape and dilatations (figs 76 and 77). A slice of a pink agate from this locality shows a lacy structure due to systematic alternating bands of quartz and chalcedony (fig 78). A further selection of fine agates from this famous locality is shown in fig 79.

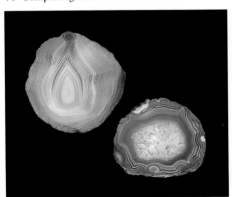

77 Agates from Path of Condie

78 Lace-like banding in agate, Path of Condie

Binn Hill, Glen Farg

This area lies some 12 kilometres south-south-east of Perth and east of the motorway. Large agates (up to 15 cm, for example) have been collected from this locality. The agates are generally blue or blue and white in colour, and occasionally contain a large proportion of amethyst or quartz. A former member of the Pentland Lapidary Society, the late Alex Ferguson of Edinburgh, picked up from one of the farm fields an agate that became a great favourite of his. He called it the 'rising sun' (fig 80). It is now in the National Museums of Scotland with many other agates from his fine collection.

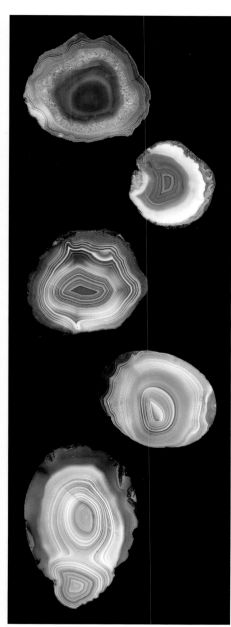

80 Alex Ferguson's 'rising sun' agate from Binn Hill

79 Agates from Path of Condie

81 *Overleaf*: detail of agate from Norman's Law

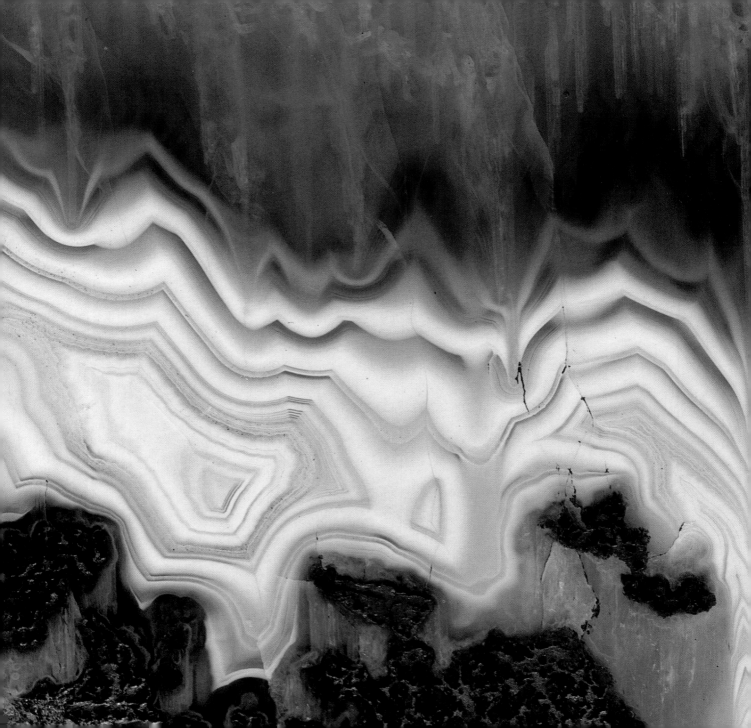

The Cupar area

The town of Cupar, on the northern side of the former county (now Region) of Fife, is the market centre for the agricultural produce of the fertile Howe of Fife. It is also a convenient base for exploring the many renowned agate localities in the hills to the north.

Norman's Law

Norman's Law is a prominent hill (285 metres high) nearly 10 kilometres north-west of Cupar. Although few agates have been found on the Law itself, some very fine blue-grey-white agates have been found, probably in the old quarries in the immediate vicinity of the Law (these are marked only on the six-inch map series published last century).

Stalactitic agates are characteristic of this locality (fig 82), but fine fortification agates also occur (fig 83). One of the latter shows a broader outer band of quartz surrounding central banded chalcedony. This agate emphasizes that although quartz is usually central to chalcedony, any order of layering is in fact possible (as Heddle long ago pointed out). The second fortification agate shows a splendid dilatation.

In fig 84, a quite extraordinary agate is shown in which pendants of blue-grey chalcedony disposed vertically suddenly bend sideways at their tips. The author knows of no comparable specimen.

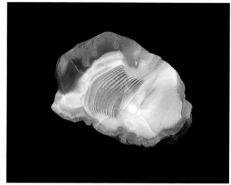

84 A unique agate from Norman's Law

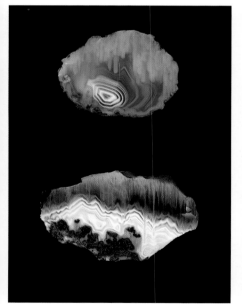

82 Stalactitic agates from Norman's Law

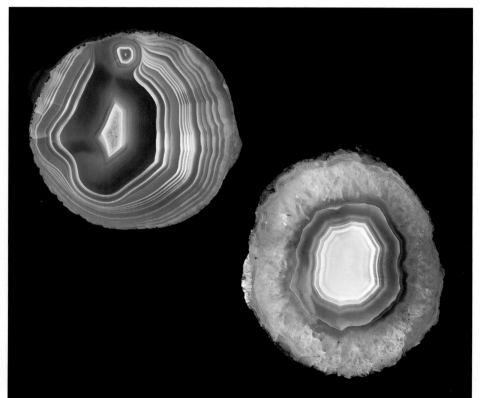

83 Fortification agates from Norman's Law

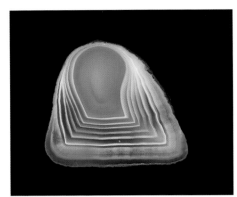

86 Agate from Balmeadowside

Balmeadowside Farm
This locality lies about 2.5 kilometres south-east of Norman's Law and is close to the Cupar-Newburgh road. Signs of agates abound in the fields around the farm and to its north, on Prospect Hill. The agates from here are commonly blue-grey in colour with prominent white bands of chalcedony, and their centres are often tinged with what Heddle called a 'rose-blush' hue (fig 85).

85 Agates from Balmeadowside

87 Agate from Balmeadowside

Luthrie

This extensive locality is about 3 kilometres east of Norman's Law. Fine agates have been collected from many fields in this area, and in Moonzie, the area extending to the south-east. M. F. Heddle listed 'Heather Hill' as a prime locality in this area, but its location is now unknown. Possibly it was to the west of Luthrie at or around Emily Hill. Agates from here, he says, are bluish with milk-white bands (fig 88). The largest agate has a central calcite crystal, which formed before the chalcedony crystallized. It is curious that the subsequent chalcedony bands did not follow around the outline of this crystal. The collection of Alex Ferguson, who specialized in collecting from this locality, shows that other coloured agates occur at Luthrie (fig 89). One of the four specimens is actually a geode, filled incompletely towards the centre by brown quartz crystals. In other examples of geodes, amethyst can replace smoky-brown quartz or exist alongside it.

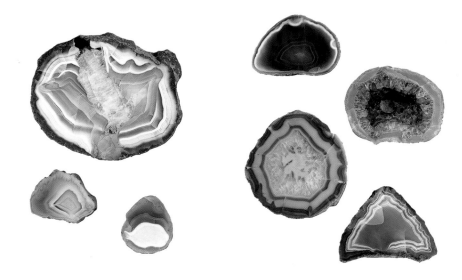

88 Agates from Luthrie

89 Agates from Luthrie

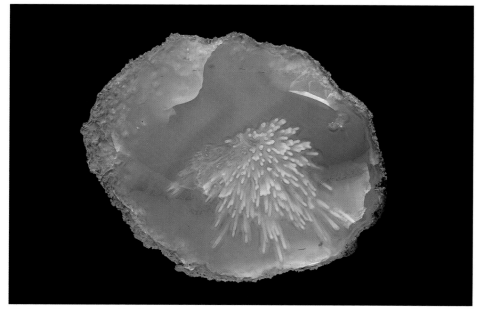

90 Sagenitic agate from Dunbog

Dunbog

This small locality situated along an old railway line some 3 kilometres south of Norman's Law yielded a number of interesting agates in the early 1970s. One of these, a sagenitic agate, a slice of which is illustrated in fig 90, shows a spray of fine chalcedony tubes which had formerly enclosed needle-shaped crystals most of which have long disappeared.

Middlefield Farm

Middlefield lies about 1.5 kilometres north-east of Cupar. Agates of brilliant yellow and red colours have been found in small numbers on the fields of the farm which is situated on sandstone rocks, so the agates are clearly not of local origin. They are quite different from most Scottish agates and are highly sought-after (figs 91 to 94).

91 Agate from Middlefield

92 Onyx agates from Middlefield

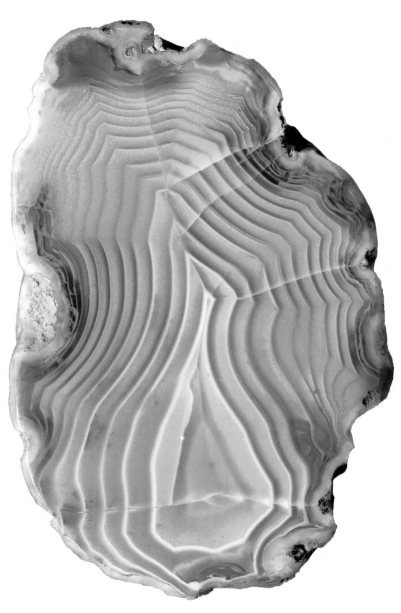

93 Agate from Middlefield

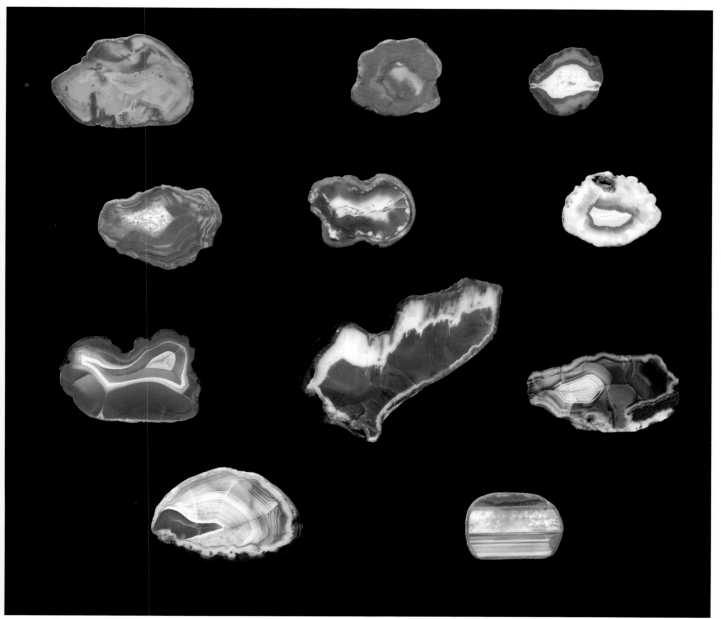

94 Agates from Middlefield

Scurr Hill, Balmerino

No account of Fife agates would be complete without mention of the attractive vein agates occurring on the west slope of Scurr Hill just to the east of Balmerino and about 5 kilometres west of the Tay Railway Bridge. Wisps of a green mineral sheathed by a pale greyish mineral (together known as the 'moss') are associated with irregular patches of colourless and grey-white chalcedony together with some reddish natrolite (a zeolite mineral) (fig 96). The structure of this moss agate as seen under a microscope is shown in fig 97.

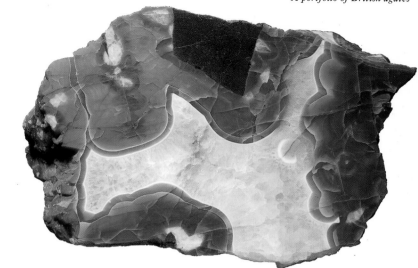

98 Carnelian agate from Tay Railway Bridge

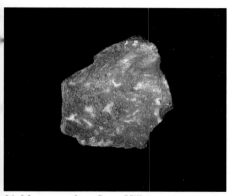

96 Moss agate from Scurr Hill

99 Moss agate from Tayport

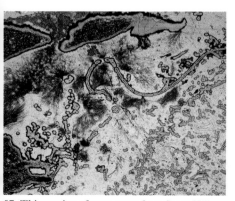

97 Thin section of moss agate from Scurr Hill

95 *Opposite*: detail of moss agate from Tayport

Tay Railway Bridge

Large blocks of carnelian agate (up to 30 cm or more) were uncovered during excavations for the Tay Railway Bridge in the 1880s. Thick bands of carnelian enclose white crystalline quartz (fig 98). Agate has also been found on the shores of the Tay, particularly on the south shore, extending from the west of Balmerino to Tayport in the east. An especially fine and rare moss agate was found last century from around Tayport (figs 95 and 99).

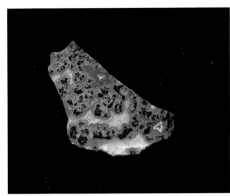

100 Vein agate from Burn Anne

The Ayr area

The town of Ayr (in the Strathclyde Region) is an attractive resort with excellent beaches and a fishing harbour on Ayr Bay. Agates have been found in Burn Anne near Galston, some 25 kilometres north-east of Ayr, and along the coastal stretch from Heads of Ayr to Dunure, some 10 to 15 kilometres to the south.

Burn Anne, Galston

This area has long been famous for its beautiful jasp agates. These are vein agates and in them patches of red, orange and yellow jasper (together with green celadonite) are associated with blue-grey or slightly violet chalcedony (fig 100). Others of similar type are associated also with white chalcedony (fig 102). Still other types consist of chalcedony surrounding stalactites of jasper which, when cut transversely, produce a variety called 'piped agate' (fig 103). The range and distribution of bright colours within these jasp agates led Heddle to write 'the specimens are altogether unrivalled in beauty'.

There is, unfortunately, no trace left of the reported early workings which occurred on both banks of the Burn Anne (north-east of Threepwood Farm). Here, within volcanic rock the vein agate occurred in brick-shaped lumps cemented together by layers of the mineral calcite. Only a few agate-hunters in recent years have been lucky enough to find a piece of this magnificent agate. Fortification agates are sometimes found loose in Burn Anne; they are quite different from the vein agate just described, and are not related to it in origin (fig 101).

101 Fortification agates from Burn Anne

103 *Opposite*: 'Piped agate' from Burn Anne

102 Vein agates from Burn Anne

Heads of Ayr to Dunure

In this area agates have been collected from beach pebble deposits or from fields inland. The agates show a wide range of colours and structure (figs 104 to 107). The oval-shaped onyx agate is one of hundreds of agates collected in recent years by Barbara Macpherson of Ayr, from beach deposits close to a well-known holiday camp. The scenic agate with much green celadonite in it is also from the Heads of Ayr. The red agate and the round onyx/quartz agate are from Dunure. An excellent guide to the agates of Heads of Ayr and Dunure is John Smith's *Semi-precious stones of Carrick* (1910). This book is richly illustrated, and provides much interesting reading.

105 Scenic agate from Heads of Ayr

104 Onyx agate from Heads of Ayr

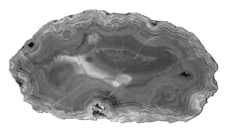

106 Agate from Dunure

107 Onyx agate from Dunure

Isles of Mull, Iona, and Rhum

Mull, Iona, and Rhum, famous centres for geological study, are islands off the west coast of Scotland. Mull and Iona are reached by passenger ferry from Oban, while Rhum is reached via Mallaig. The lavas occurring in parts of Mull and Rhum are different from the andesite lavas of the Old Red Sandstone of the Midland Valley of Scotland, and, as they belong to the Tertiary era, are also much younger in geological age. The type of volcanic rock occurring in these islands is basalt, and these lavas contain fewer agates than the andesite lavas of the mainland. They are rarely coloured other than a blue-grey-white. There has, however, been less of a search made for agates in these islands than in the localities previously discussed.

Ross of Mull

Blue-grey agates up to some 15 cm across have been found *in situ* at Port Nan Droigheann on the south coast of Mull. These agates sometimes carry early-formed brown calcite crystals (fig 108). Other Mull agates have a pale honey tint and are characterized by whorls consisting of fan-shaped quartz crystal groups alternating with curved bands of white or grey-white chalcedony (fig 109). Of agate localities in Mull, Jock Nimlin, the doyen collector of Mull agates, says in his interesting booklet *Let's look at Scottish gemstones* (1974):

> Unfortunately for people with little experience in rock-scrambling and cross-country walking in rough terrain, the Mull locations are in fairly remote places. There is no road along the south coast of the island, although the coastline can be reached by car at Carsaig and Loch Buie. Other localities on the west coast at Ardmeanach and the coastline north of Loch na Keal are also

difficult to reach. Therefore large exposures of the Mull lavas still await investigation by collectors.

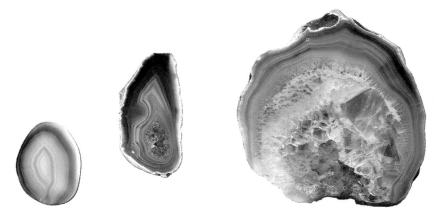

108 Agates from Mull

109 'Whorl agate' from Mull

Iona

Blue-grey-white agates, usually 2 to 3 cm in size, are found on Iona beaches.
Occasionally a larger one is found, such as that presented to the National Museums of Scotland in 1896; more rarely, coloured agates of the jasp or moss type are also found (fig 110). As Iona has no agate-bearing lavas, the agates on the beach are thought to have come from Mull, carried long ago on moving ice. If so, there must be a source of coloured agates on Mull.

111 Agate from Rhum

110 Agate and jasp agates from Iona

Rhum

The Revd Dr John Walker, Professor of Natural History, University of Edinburgh (1779–1803), was one of the first people to point out that agates could be collected from the shores of this island, particularly on its north-east and northern coastlines. Rhum is not easy to visit as the island is managed solely as a nature reserve by its owners, the Nature Conservancy Council. Its only inhabitants are members of the Council's staff. Collecting is not allowed on Rhum without permission from their Inverness headquarters.

Agates have also been found on the beaches below Bloodstone Hill on the western side of the island. They are blue-grey-white and are much like those on Mull and Iona (fig 111). They are probably derived from the Tertiary lavas forming much of Bloodstone Hill (Sgor Mhor).

112 *Opposite*: detail of jasp agate from the Cheviot Hills

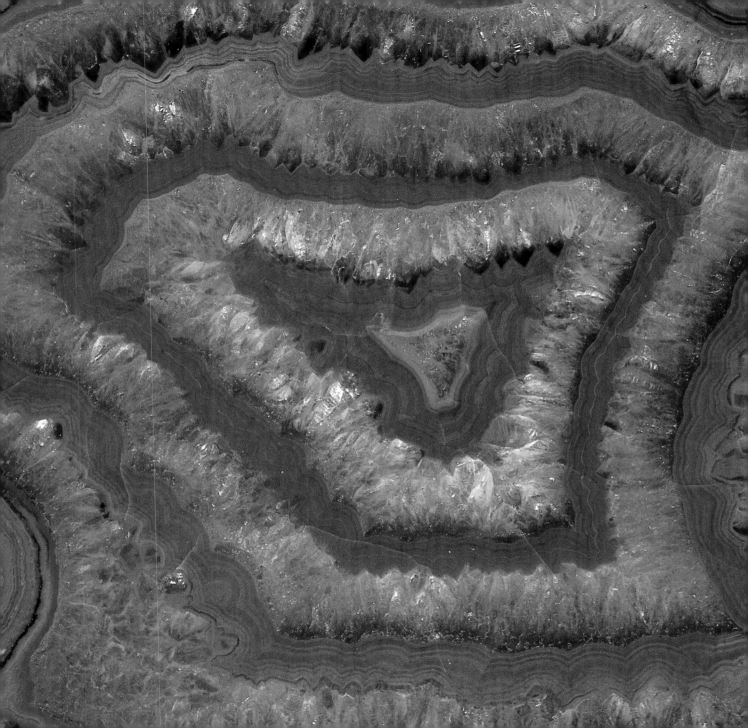

Agates from England, Wales, and Ireland

Agates are not as plentiful in England, Wales, and Ireland as they are in Scotland, primarily because agate-bearing lavas are more scarce. In Northern Ireland, for example, extensive lavas exist (mainly in Antrim) but these are Tertiary lavas which appear rarely to carry agates. Agates are even more scarce in Eire. In Wales, agate-bearing volcanics are found on rare occasions in the Ordovician basalts near Builth Wells, Powys, but the agates are small and of inferior quality.

In England there is a large area of agate-bearing rocks of Old Red Sandstone age in Northumberland, in the Cheviot Hills which straddle the England-Scotland border. Elsewhere in England small agates occur sporadically in other volcanic rocks, for example in the Lake District and Derbyshire.

In England and Wales most agates are found loose in beach shingle. These agates are not generally of local origin, but are by-products of the effects of glaciation within Britain. Glacial scouring of the land has produced various kinds of residual loose rock deposits such as the widespread boulder–clay – a deposit consisting of pebbles enclosed in a clay matrix. Such deposits are found near or at many English coasts because some of the glaciers in the last Ice Age travelled south from Scotland and northern England and shed their loads when they melted in the south of England. Boulder-clay is a soft rock and is easily disintegrated by weathering, allowing pebbles (some of which are agates) to be washed out and accumulate on beaches. These pebbles have not always remained where they were weathered out, but have been moved along the shores (often many kilometres in distance) by the sea. This is because winds blow waves against these shores at an angle, thus liberating part of the waves' energies to move the pebbles slowly sideways along the coast.

Beach deposits are interesting because the agates found in them are associated with other attractive pebbles. An excellent account of such deposits has been given in Clarence Ellis's book *The pebbles on the beach* (1954). His book also lists and describes a number of productive beach deposits. If you want to find out if there is a shingle beach in or near your coastal area, the best source of information is the One-Inch or 1:50 000 series of the Ordnance Survey maps of Great Britain. Some modern road atlases also have pebble beaches marked on them.

Cheviot Hills agates

The agate-bearing region of the Cheviot Hills lies roughly between the towns of Carter Bar and Wooler (east-west), and Coldstream and Rothbury (north-south). The rocks forming the hills consist of Old Red Sandstone volcanics and granite, the latter forming The Cheviot itself. These rocks are largely covered over by coarse grass and some heather so rock outcrops are rare. The agates may be found loose in any of the many rivers and streams which radiate from the higher reaches of the hills, as well as in the fields which surround the lower slopes of the Cheviots. Rock screes on some of the hills or cliffs may also be productive. The Cheviots in general have not been fully exploited by the agate-hunter.

Cheviot agates are often large, up to 15 or 20 cm in diameter. They are characteristically coloured in startling shades of red or yellow-brown, often associated with bluish-grey agate (figs 113, 114 and 115). A superb but rare type of Cheviot agate is that containing concentric bands of brilliant jasp agate alternating with bands of crystalline quartz (fig 112). Such an agate could only have formed by the chemical differentiation of a hydrous silica gel in association with the segregation by diffusion of its pigmenting constituents. A fine example of a Cheviot agate showing the clear chalcedony layer, chalcedony banding, central quartz crystals, a tube of escape and dilatation was found by Tom Barker of West Baldon, South Tyneside (fig 116).

As mentioned above, agates occur on a number of English and Welsh beaches, and two examples are illustrated here. The first is a collection of carnelian pebbles, from Cley beach on the north coast of Norfolk, which have been tumble-polished (fig 117). The second example is a slice of flint pebble from the beach at Hastings, East Sussex, the outer zone only of which consists of greyish banded agate (fig 118). The large and striking reddish 'potato-stones' found in some of the fields bordering the north and south slopes of the Mendip Hills in Somerset occur in a sedimentary rock of Triassic age (fig 119). An agate from Cheddar is shown in fig 120. Greyish-white vein agate of poor quality has been found in Cornwall (fig 121).

Much work remains to be done in the compilation of an accurate and comprehensive inventory of agates from England, Wales, and Ireland.

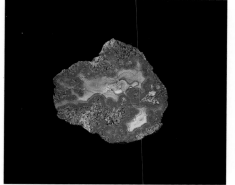

113 Agate from Cheviot Hills

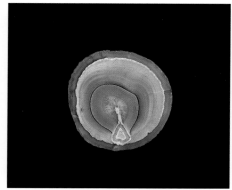

116 Tube of escape; dilatation, Cheviot agate

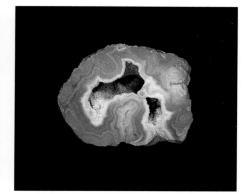

119 'Potato-stone' from Mendip Hills

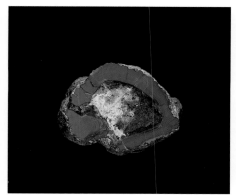

114 Agate from Cheviot Hills

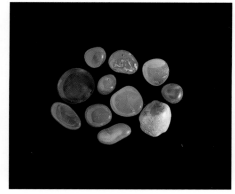

117 Tumbled carnelian pebbles, Cley beach

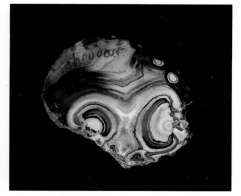

120 Agate from Cheddar

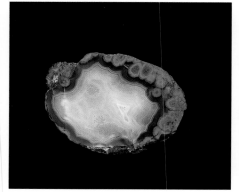

115 Agate from Cheviot Hills

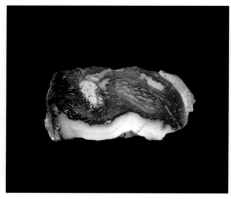

118 Slice of flint pebble from beach at Hastings

121 Vein agate from Cornwall

122 Agate-hunters (beginners) searching a beach for agates

Collecting agates

Agates have been collected for practical and ornamental purposes since the beginning of civilization. In Scotland, agates of native origin have been found in a prehistoric cairn at Cairnhill, Monquhitter, Aberdeenshire, and from a middle stone-age occupation site at Morton, Fife, some 7000 to 9000 years old, where small edge tools (scrapers) have been discovered (fig 123). An agate talisman, or charm stone, possibly dating back to Roman times has been found in a farm field at Newstead, Roxburghshire (fig 124).

Some countries, such as Egypt, India, China and Sumer (now part of Iraq) exploited agates commercially. In Egypt, for example, agates were collected from the deserts as early as 3500 BC, while in Sumer (one of the world's earliest civilizations) agates were fashioned into beads, cylinder seals and signet rings. Long before Christ the Arabians traded in agate believed to have come from India. The Greek philosopher and founder of botanical science, Theophrastus (*c.* 372–286 BC) believed that agate was first found in Sicily near a river called Achates. The Roman naturalist, Pliny the Elder (*c.* AD 23–79) tells us that it was a mark of the highest prestige to own a cup made of agate. Both these writers have recorded tales of the talismanic qualities of agates. They were believed to have the power to cure the sting of poisonous spiders, to turn away tempests, or to make a wrestler invincible.

In Europe the great centre for agates has been in the German town of Idar-Oberstein, some 130 kilometres south-west of Frankfurt. Here, for hundreds of years, agates were found in commercial quantities in the hills surrounding the dual-town. Thousands of people were employed in the trade of gem-cutting, and vast quantities of fashioned agates were exported to all parts of

123 Agate and agate scraper from prehistoric sites in Scotland

124 Talisman from (possible) Roman site, Scotland

125 Old-time method of gem-cutting in Idar-Oberstein

the world (fig 125). However, by about 1860 the local agate supplies began to peter out, causing the citizens of Idar-Oberstein to search for outside sources of supply. Eventually these were found in Uruguay and Brazil from where immense numbers of agates were sent back to Idar for processing.

Agate enthusiasts should visit this charming city where all aspects of the lapidary art can be seen. Visitors will be greatly stimulated by what they see in its museums and gem-dealer's shops.

126 The town of Idar-Oberstein

Although agates were collected in Scotland in the eighteenth and nineteenth centuries, the current popularity of agate collecting in the British Isles has been much influenced by the craze that began in America during the 1930s. According to Lelande Quick, author of *The book of agates* (1963):

> Present day rockhounding, and the enormous business it has generated, is really a child of the Depression in the 1930s. Many people who were unemployed tramped the hills and valleys of California in search of more gold, and they brought home with them finds of petrified wood and interesting rocks, which had a ready sale in curio shops where they were marketed as so-called 'Indian jewelry'. Gradually there came an exchange of information among individuals about localities, and finally groups for study and collecting were formed.

According to Lelande Quick, the United States Bureau of Mines estimated that in 1959 there were approximately three million amateur rock collectors in the United States. Magazines were published to cater for the needs of such collectors, and one of the earliest and best of these, founded and edited by Peter Zodac (1894–1967) in 1926, is *Rocks and Minerals* which is still being published today (fig 127).

127 Peter Zodac, founder and first editor of *Rocks and Minerals* (1926–67)

There are no hard and fast rules for starting an agate collection, but it is wise to seek advice from an experienced collector. The following guidelines should be noted:

1 A beginner must know what an agate looks like in the field, and must be able to recognize an agate enclosed in volcanic rock or found loose as a pebble in a ploughed field or in beach shingle.

2 When the beginner cannot immediately contact an experienced collector he should contact the curator of his nearest natural history or geological museum and ask to see specimens of raw, uncut agates, or he can check with members of the nearest gem and mineral club. The colour illustrations in this book should also help.

3 The precise details of an agate occurrence should be ascertained before it is visited, since hours can be wasted looking for a locality described in only general terms such as 'that field near East Neuk farm'. The beginner must know precisely which field it is: is it north, south, east or west of the farm, for example? A map grid reference number should be obtained, if possible, from someone who has collected from the locality.

4 The nature of the agate-bearing rocks in the area should be confirmed by checking this on a one-inch or 1:50 000 geological map (published by the British Geological Survey). Articles in magazines or geological memoirs which describe the occurrence of agates at the chosen locality are useful; the aim is to collect all helpful information before setting out.

The new collector will require the following equipment: one or two small geological hammers of different weights, one of about 1 kg (2 lbs) and one of about 2 kg (4 lbs); one or two cold chisels of different weights and lengths; an eye-lens of 8–10 powers of magnification; bags or sacks in which to put the collected agates, and a rucksack in which

to transport them (fig 128). The following can be added: a crowbar or wrecking bar, a pick-axe, and a sledge hammer to split up large boulders containing agates. As far as field clothes are concerned, any robust casual wear that is warm and shower-proof is suitable, with a pair of walking boots, a pair of wellington boots together with thick socks, and one or two pairs of strong gloves. Finally, a large folding-knife, permanent black marker pens, string and cardboard boxes are useful extras.

In proceeding to and operating at a locality a collector should comply with certain safety and conservation rules:

Agates (or other geological specimens) must not be collected from sites on private property without the owner's permission.
Collecting should not be done in fields where crops are growing.
Gates should be closed; care should be taken when lighting fires; and litter must not be left behind.
On entering quarries and similar areas a protective hard-hat must be worn. Goggles should be worn when smashing up lumps of hard rock with heavy hammers to protect the eyes from flying splinters.
When collecting or hammering at the base of cliffs or steep rock piles, a collector must look out for possible sudden movement or falls of rock that may cause injury.
If a new find of agate-bearing rock is made, only part of the spoil should be taken, as something should be left for future agate collectors.
Notes of the precise localities from which agates have been collected should be made. The minimum data should be recorded on a label enclosed in each sack or bag of specimens giving the grid-reference number of the locality, date of collecting, and any other relevant data. In the days that follow the collector should sort out his treasures carefully. Poor specimens

should be discarded and the best numbered and listed. Specimens can be numbered by writing directly on them with permanent marker pen, or by writing the number on a short length of adhesive zinc oxide tape attached to the specimen.

A useful and inexpensive book on this subject is *Fossils, minerals and rocks, collection and preservation* by R. Croucher and A. R. Woolley (1982). Collectors are also strongly recommended to obtain copies of the following leaflets – all available free on application to the Geologists' Association,

Burlington House, Piccadilly, London:
A Code for Geological Field Work.
Geologists' Association.
Rocks, Fossils and Minerals: how to make the most of your collection. Geological Curators' Group: Geological Society.
Code of Practice for Geological visits to Quarries, Mines and Caves. Institution of Geologists.

128 Collecting equipment

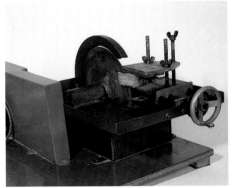

129 Slicing an agate

132 Grinding a slice (into cabochon form)

135 Polishing a cabochon

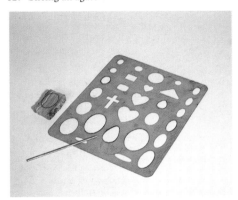

130 Scribing a slice

133 Sanding a cabochon

136 Lapping an agate slice

131 Trimming a slice

134 Polishing a cabochon

137 A tumbler and mounted tumbled stones

Cutting and polishing agates

The collecting and fashioning of agates have existed side by side since the days of the earliest civilizations. Those who fashion agates and other stones are called lapidaries from the Latin *lapis, -idis,* a stone. The process of shaping rough gemstones is called lapidary.

Most lapidaries were professionals until about 1800 from when, in Western Europe, there was a slow but steady increase in the number of amateurs. Until the 1930s the number of amateurs compared to professionals was small, owing to the lack of easily obtained equipment and instructional books. None the less such necessities existed for those determined enough to seek them out, as is exemplified by the delightful coloured illustration in fig 138, taken from the book *Familiar lessons on mineralogy and geology* by John Mawe, an English mineralogist (3rd edition, London, 1821). In a chapter dealing with lapidary procedures, Mawe begins:

> The agreeable amusement of collecting Pebbles, Jaspers, Agates, etc. has of late become so fashionable, that almost everyone who visits the coast has been employed in searching for these pretty productions, and forming collections of them; but great disappointment has frequently taken place, owing to the want of a convenient method of cutting and polishing these beautiful substances. To obviate which, a Portable Mill has been contrived, so as to render the operation easy, and which will afford both instructive and agreeable employment.

Mawe ends his chapter with these words:

> The expense of this Apparatus, with Emery, Putty, etc. is from six to eight guineas, according as it is fitted up for various purposes. Some are made as high as ten pounds. It is particularly recommended that those who make use of them, should see a practitioner perform all the operations, by way of instruction.

138 Home lapidary equipment, early 19th century

Interest in amateur lapidary has had its ups and downs. In the early part of this century little interest was shown but during the 1930s and 1940s the collecting of gemstones and other minerals reached craze proportions, especially in North America. This was mainly due to advances in technology meeting the great demand by mineral collectors for suitable tools to cut open their specimens. Cutting agates revealed inner pictures of coloured perfection and striking structures. New equipment eased the often laborious procedures of older lapidary techniques, and along with the production and sale of lapidary equipment came books of self-help and instruction on how to use the equipment. Gem and lapidary clubs sprang up in their hundreds, there being a need not only to share the use of equipment but also the pleasure of collecting and fashioning stones.

The equipment needed by a lapidary and the basic steps in gem-making are best illustrated by outlining the procedure by which a cabochon is made. A cabochon is a stone which is rounded on the top and flat on the back, without facets.

The first step is for the lapidary to select a piece of gemstone rough, in this case an uncut lace agate. A slab or slice of this agate is now required. This is obtained by using a power-driven diamond saw whose blade consists of a circular metal disc, the rim of which is impregnated with crushed diamonds. The agate is held in a vice and then pushed against the rotating saw blade which cuts into it (fig 129). Having obtained a slice from the agate the lapidary scribes it, sketching out on it the shape he requires. He does this with a sharp bronze or aluminium pencil, and he may use a manufactured template cut to the shape(s) required to make the task easier (fig 130).

The next step is to cut or trim away all unwanted material from the scribed slab, and the lapidary uses the diamond saw to do this (fig 131). In the next stage the trimmed slice is first stuck onto a dopping stick using dopping wax. Dopping is a convenient method of holding the stone while it is being ground on wet abrasive wheels. These wheels are made of silicon carbide, and fine and coarse varieties are necessary (fig 132). Next comes the sanding stage, in which the scratches left after grinding are removed. This can be done in a variety of ways; the sanding device shown here is called a drum-sander (fig 133).

The final stage is the polishing which is done on a buff with a mixture of polishing powder and water. It is best to have two or three buffs, one for each polishing agent of choice as, for example, tin oxide, cerium oxide, or even the somewhat messy jeweller's rouge, an oxide of iron (fig 134).

Another common procedure is to cut an agate in half and polish one or both surfaces. Making such 'polished flats' involves a process known as lapping where a lapping machine is used to grind, sand, and polish. If this is a universal type of machine the grinding laps, sanding discs and polishing buffs are interchangeable. In the grinding stage the lapidary can use loose grits (grains of silicon carbide) with water on cast iron laps or he can use diamond impregnated copper plates which do away with messy grits (fig 136).

Yet another procedure, and one that is easy to accomplish, is tumbling. Tumbled stones are produced when pieces of hard stones (broken agates or beach pebbles for example) are placed inside a round or hexagonal container with water and abrasive grits. The container, or barrel, is usually power-driven and has to rotate or 'tumble' its load for two or three weeks continuously. In the process, however, several grades of grit (from coarse to fine) are used but in the final stage a polishing agent, such as cerium oxide, must be used. The result, if the original stones have been carefully selected for hardness, is normally a pile of glowing stones all ready to be turned into pendants and bracelets by applying simple manufactured mounts to the stones using special adhesives (fig 137). There are many other procedures in lapidary, for example carving, sphere making and mosaic work.

A considerable number of books on gem-cutting are now available. Check your nearest library, the craft sections in bookshops, or write to the Gemmological Association of Great Britain, 2 Carey Lane, London EC2V 8AB, who maintain an extensive bookshop. A number of magazines dealing with lapidary and gemstones have come and gone, but the *Lapidary Journal,* first published in 1947, is one of the best available and can be ordered from *Lapidary Journal* inc., 1094 Cudahy Place, San Diego, California 92110. This periodical is published monthly and contains articles on many gem minerals including agate. Libraries with a good mineralogical section would probably subscribe to this journal.

Dealers in rough gemstones, lapidary equipment and the like commonly produce catalogues listing the availability and prices of their wares. These catalogues, often well illustrated, are usually available at a modest charge, and some may be free on application. For the names and addresses of dealers and manufacturing firms check the well-known annual *Rockhound Buyers Guide,* published every April by the *Lapidary Journal.* There is no equivalent British guide, but a list of current lapidary dealers is contained in the Trade Directory of the British Lapidary and Mineral Dealers Association.

Displays of minerals, gems, lapidary and gemmological equipment are held several times a year in the UK, usually in hotels. They are well worth visiting as a whole range of products is conveniently displayed in one venue. Displays are also held on the Continent, particularly in Munich and Paris.

A few museums display collections of both raw and fashioned agates. These will usually be found in the geology, natural history or art sections. Examples are the British Museum (Natural History), London; the Geological Museum, London, and the National Museums of Scotland, Edinburgh. In many towns, evening classes sponsored by local authorities sometimes include courses in geology and lapidary. Your local gem, mineral or lapidary club may be helpful, so contact them and ask if it is possible to look at their gem-cutting equipment. You may be able to talk to people who have mastered the lapidary procedures, which is probably the best source of help and information, as well as being an inspiration to attempt cutting and polishing yourself.

139 Agate and chalcedony cups, agate marbles and a slice of agate from the collection of William Hunter (1718–83)

140 Head of distinctly banded agate: French

141 Small-sword with silver belt and agate grip: English, 1720

143 Beckford Cup, made from agate with silver-gilt mounts, mark of Joseph Angell: London, 1815–16

142 *Left*: bowl made from dyed agate, associated with crystalline quartz mounted in ormolu. Presented to the Geological Museum by Mrs E. Warne

144 Cameo bust of a lady: Haitian, 16th century

145 Chinese snuff bottle of moss agate

146 Bowl made from naturally coloured agate

147 Workbox, inlaid with polished 'Scotch Pebbles'

Pebble Jewellery

Pebble jewellery is the name given to articles of jewellery made in Scotland since the beginning of the nineteenth century. Small pieces of agate with some other stones (for example, jasper, bloodstone, cairngorm, and granite) are set in mosaic patterns in brooches with silver or gold mounts. Such jewellery achieved great popularity, and consequently was copied and made in Birmingham, Devon, and elsewhere, sometimes using local materials rather than stones from Scotland.

The spread of the use of Scottish agates in jewellery and other fashioned objects probably kept pace with the spread of knowledge of where natural agate might be found. Certainly several localities were known by the mid-eighteenth century, for example Usan in Angus, Kinnoull Hill near Perth, and the shores of the island of Rhum.

Pebble jewellery has not always been in vogue. Probably the most popular period (excluding the current period since the early 1960s) was during Queen Victoria's reign (1837–1901). The Queen's love of Balmoral and the surrounding region led to an increased interest in pebble jewellery. She was interested in 'cairngorms' – brown transparent crystals of quartz, which occurred in the Cairngorm Mountains and Lochnagar. Queen Victoria ascended Beinn à Bhuird (a mountain some 1200 metres high and about 30 kilometres west of Balmoral) on 6 September 1850, and managed to find a number of cairngorm crystals from among the rocks of the summit plateau. She records the event in her book *Leaves from the Journal of our Life in the Highlands* (1868).

In Scotland most of the lapidaries making pebble jewellery lived and worked in Edinburgh. Often their workshops, like those of their associated craftsmen (the

working jeweller, the gold and silversmiths) were situated in back streets in the New Town and were dingy, smoky places. Yet by about 1870 the number of people working gold, silver and precious stones in Scotland has been estimated to be 'little short of two thousand, and a large proportion of these are employed in Edinburgh'. Pebble jewellery declined in popularity just before World War I until its revival just after World War II. The last lapidary from the old school in Edinburgh was Alexander Begbie, who died at the age of 83 in 1958.

A selection of typical 'Scotch Pebble Jewellery' and an inlaid workbox from the collections of the National Museums of Scotland are shown in figs 147 and 148. An unusual piece of agate jewellery, from the collection of the British Museum (Natural History) is shown in fig 149. It may be from Australia or New Zealand. Examples of agate artefacts from different parts of the

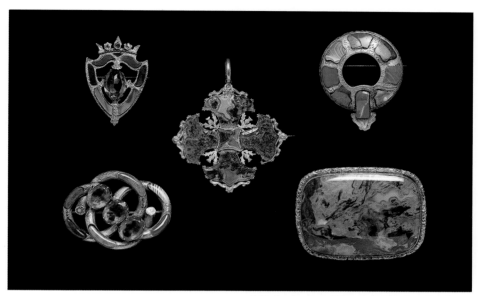

148 A selection of 'Scotch Pebble Jewellery'

world, some reflecting beliefs in agate's magical powers, are shown in figs 139 to 146.

150 *Overleaf*: Amethystine 'eye agate' from Brazil

149 Scenic agate pendant (not Scottish)

Agates around the world

Although agates are found in many countries, they are rarely found in substantial quantities. Occasionally deposits are so large that they have been developed on a commercial scale.

The world's largest and most productive deposit of agate-bearing rocks lies in a mountain chain some 600 kilometres in length, extending from Porto Alegre in the state of Rio Grande do Sul, in southern Brazil, westwards to the region of Salto on the Uruguay river in Uruguay. The agate-bearing rocks are highly altered amygdaloidal basic lavas.

The agates are found loose on the ground or in the beds of streams and rivers and are often huge, sometimes reaching 2 metres in diameter. Although a flesh-red colour is rather frequently seen in Brazilian agates, many of them are a dingy, unattractive bluish-grey or pale brown. Such agate, however, possesses a distinct advantage over agate from other lands as it can be coloured artificially. Treatments to colour agate include heating, irradiation, bleaching, colour impregnation, and dyeing. The methods currently available are summarized by Kurt Nassau in his book *Gemstone enhancement* (1984). Samples of artificially coloured agate are shown at the top of this page. The occurrence of agate and associated quartz minerals in Brazil is said to have been discovered in the last century by a native of Oberstein in Germany. Huge amounts of agate have since been exported to Germany for cutting and polishing. However, since the last World War, Brazil itself has gradually established a strong and flourishing gemstone industry which deals with a host of gemstones including agate.

A few examples of Brazilian agate are now given. Note that the term 'Brazilian agate' is generally used for agates coming from Brazil and Uruguay. In the first example, a

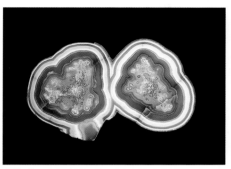

151 Concentric-banded agate from Brazil

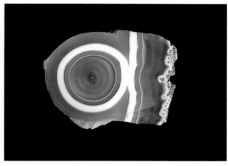

152 Banding in Brazilian agate

brownish agate, concentric layers of chalcedony enclose a central area containing tubes of banded chalcedony intimately associated with crystalline quartz (fig 151). In the second example amethyst crystals encrusting layers of whitish chalcedony have been cut from a protruberance to expose an 'eye' of white chalcedony, resulting in a most attractive specimen (fig 150). The next example shows a pale brown agate which has been sliced to expose a circular band of white chalcedony sitting on a horizontal white band. The finely banded structure that is so characteristic of all agates is clearly shown (fig 152). The final example of Brazilian agate is interesting in that it shows how different an agate can look depending on how or where it is cut open. The slice illustrated (fig 153) is only 1.5 cm thick, yet one side shows onyx totally enclosed by chalcedony, while the other side shows the same onyx extending to the outer surface of the agate, via a tube of escape. It is important to realize that an agate's structure cannot be fully understood until the agate is cut open in at least two directions, perpendicular to each other, and the resulting exposed features can be visualized in three dimensions.

153 Variation in structural pattern in thick agate slice from Brazil

As already mentioned, important deposits of agate have been worked for hundreds of years in the neighbourhood of Idar-Oberstein, but agate also occurs in other areas of Germany. A most interesting deposit was found in 1750 at Schlottwitz, near Wesenstein, in the Muglitz valley in Saxony, where it occurred as veins filling fissures of rocks. According to Max Bauer in his book *Precious stones* (1904), Schlottwitz agate has narrow, brightly coloured bands arranged parallel to the surfaces of the vein, and contains, besides agate, common chalcedony, jasper, quartz and amethyst. At a certain spot the material of half of the vein has been completely broken up by earth movements. The angular fragments of agate thus produced were afterwards cemented together by amethyst and ordinary clear quartz – the resulting stone being known as brecciated agate (fig 155).

The second German agate illustrated is from the amygdaloidal volcanic rocks near Idar-Oberstein. This has a narrow clear chalcedony layer, followed by a broader layer coloured yellowish by a multitude of tiny yellow iron-oxide spheres, then bands of bluish-grey and white chalcedony, ending up finally with central quartz. At least four small tubes of escape (with dilatations as well) can be seen emanating from the central quartz to, or through, the clear chalcedony layer (fig 156).

A selection of Brazilian agates fashioned in Idar-Oberstein (tazzas, bowls, ashtray, egg, earrings, etc) is shown in fig 154.

In India agates occur in amygdaloidal volcanic rocks which cover an area of some half a million square kilometres in the Deccan Plateau. The agates, which are set free by weathering of the lavas, are found loose on the ground or as pebbles in rivers flowing through the Deccan. Commercial deposits of agates are, however, found only in a few places and here they occur in thick

154 Agates fashioned in Idar-Oberstein

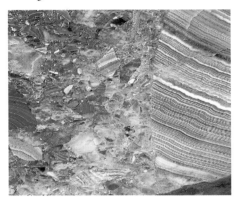

155 Brecciated agate from Schlottwitz

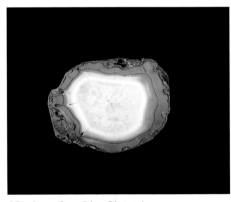

156 Agate from Idar-Oberstein

beds of Tertiary conglomerate, a sedimentary rock whose agate pebbles were derived from the weathering of amygdaloids. The best-known deposits are at Ratanpur where for some 2000 years the lapidaries at Broach (some 650 kilometres north of Bombay) obtained their supplies of rough agate. The agates are mined from the conglomerate rock by the excavation of pits which commonly measure about 1.5 metres across by 50 metres deep. Agate of poor colour is baked in earthen pots, which intensifies the colouring of the bands. The town of Cambay, to the north of Broach, was, in medieval times, a large market-place for Indian agates destined for different parts of the world.

Fine moss agates are found in India. These are agates which are generally devoid of visible banding but display instead branching inclusions (usually of a black, brown or green colour) in common chalcedony and which have a fancied resemblance to plant life such as trees, ferns, moss, shrubs, etc. (fig 157). Another type of Indian agate frequently seen in museum collections is stalactitic agate, which can display many different appearances according to how it is cut – as in fig 158, for example.

South Africa and some neighbouring countries have supplied well-known varieties of agates of which lace agate is perhaps a favourite example (fig 159). The name originates, of course, from the complex lace-like banding which this agate, popular for tumbling, shows.

The United States of America has produced some fine agates from numerous localities such as the Keweenaw Peninsula, South Dakota, and perhaps especially Oregon where the famous 'thunder eggs' are found in rhyolitic lavas and welded tuffs. These 'thunder eggs' (fig 160) often show in section a pointed structure reminiscent of a

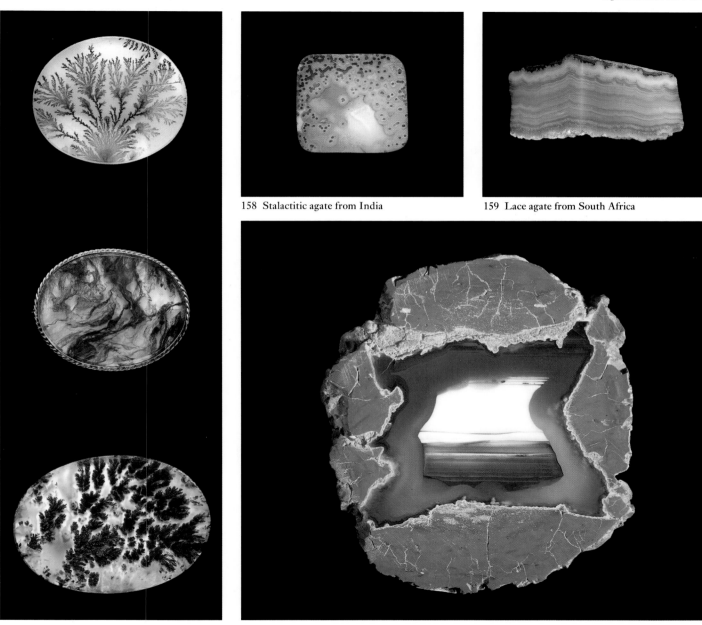

158 Stalactitic agate from India

159 Lace agate from South Africa

157 Moss agates from India

160 Thunder egg agate from Oregon

star. According to Lelande Quick, the name 'thunder eggs' comes from a popular belief among the Warm Spring Indians of Central Oregon that the concretions were missiles from the volcanoes of the Cascade Mountains, thrown whenever the gods inhabiting the mountains became angry. Thunder egg agates come mainly from central Oregon around the town of Prineville, Crook County.

Mexico has produced a number of excellent agates some of which display strongly coloured bands. Mexican agates come mainly from the north of the country midway between El Paso (in Texas, USA) and Chihuahua in Mexico. Localities are concentrated around such towns as Villa Ahumada, Moctezuma and Ojo de Laguna. One of the best known types of Mexican agate is Laguna agate (fig 161). Other notable types are Apache agate, crazy lace agate, Moctezuma agate and Coyamito agate. Agates from Mexico and the United States of America have been documented in Lieper's booklet called *The agates of North America*, published in 1966 by the *Lapidary Journal*. Unfortunately most of the agate illustrations are in black and white.

Agates from Morocco are not well known, but a fine fortification agate showing greyish-white chalcedonic banding, and said to come from the desert near Erfoud, south of Ksar es Souk, was presented some years ago to the National Museums of Scotland. It shows a fine tube of escape and dilatation (fig 162).

Australia has provided agate-hunters with a fine source at Agate Creek, some 80 kilometres south of the town Forsayth in northern Queensland. An agate from this volcanic region was recently presented to the National Museums of Scotland and is shown here (fig 163). Agates from this locality are well illustrated in a booklet by Hap Wheeley entitled *Take your pick to Agate Creek*, published in 1976.

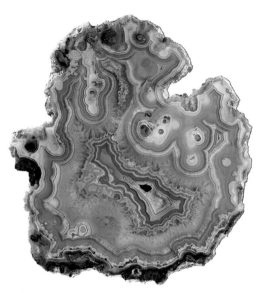

161 Laguna agate from Mexico

Agates of many sizes and varieties (some most strange) have been found in the Clent Hills, in the Canterbury district of the South Island of New Zealand. A large collection of these agates was presented to the National Museums of Scotland in 1915. One of them shows in particular very distinct segregation banding (fig 164). Each of these whitish bands is also lined on its inner side by tiny teeth-like quartz crystals.

162 Fortification agate from Morocco

163 Agate from Agate Creek, Australia

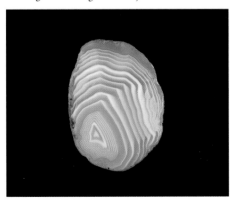

164 Agate from Clent Hills, New Zealand

Glossary

Agate banding. The most visible banding in agates is the coloured banding due to the segregation of its pigmenting impurities, for example iron oxide producing reddish tints. But this banding is not as fundamental to agate as is the systematic growth banding associated with the spherulitic crystallization of chalcedony in the clear chalcedony layer and the relatively longer fibrous growths of chalcedony in the rest of the agate. Both types of crystallization are associated with sector zoning (figs 38 and 40).

Agate dyke. In this book an agate dyke is the name given to a minutely raised lineation that commonly occurs on the exterior of agates. It is the surface expression of a rent in the clear chalcedony layer through which a small amount of nascent agate has been expelled from within some agates. An agate dyke is not usually seen on abraded agates or on agates with thick skins. Dykes can be obvious but are usually subtle features best seen with a binocular microscope and illuminated with sidelighting. Once recognized they are quickly discernible in other agates. They may sometimes run nearly all the way round an agate from near one tube of escape to another.

Agate names. There is no agreed way of spelling agate names. Some names are hyphenated, others are not. All agate names in this book are written without a hyphen.

Brecciated agate: agate which has been broken into angular fragments and later recemented by silica solutions.

Carnelian agate: agate consisting, in whole or part, of carnelian – which is a translucent red or orange-red variety of chalcedony, pale to deep in shade, containing iron impurities.

Concentric agate: agate showing circular banding in a sliced section.

Eye agate: in this book an eye agate is one showing one or more areas of concentric bands of alternating colours situated at or near the exterior surface of the agate and which are the visible exposure of hemi agate, *qv*.

Fortification agate: an agate having angular markings or parallel zigzag bands resembling the plan of a fortification.

Hemi agate: hemi agates are small hemispherical masses found on the inside wall of the clear chalcedony layer. They usually display alternating colour bands, *cf* eye agate.

Jasp agate: a mixture of jasper (an opaque chalcedony) and chalcedony, in which the jasper (characteristically red in colour) predominates.

Lace agate: an agate which has a lacy effect in its patterns.

Laguna agate: an agate from Laguna Ranch situated at Ojo de Laguna, Chihuahua, Mexico.

Moss agate: in Scotland, an agate containing inclusions of any colour (but usually green) arranged in moss-like or fern-like patterns. Most moss agate in Scotland is vein agate.

Onyx agate: a banded agate with straight parallel bands of white and different tones of grey.

Sagenitic agate: agate containing sprays of acicular crystals (usually zeolites in Scotland) which have been coated by chalcedony. The colour of these sprays is commonly pinkish-red or greyish-white.

Scenic agate: an agate with markings which form fanciful resemblances to landscapes, seascapes, etc.

Stalactitic agate: agate in which pendants (generally enclosing stringers of celadonite) have developed within the clear chalcedony layer and which hang down from that part of the clear chalcedony layer occupying the dome or top of the agate.

Thunder egg: agate from Central Oregon, USA, sections of which often show a pointed or star-like shape.

Vein agate: agate filling fissures or cracks in various types of rock.

Amygdale. A gas cavity or vesicle in a volcanic rock, which is filled with secondary minerals, such as calcite, quartz, chalcedony, or a zeolite.

Amygdaloid. A lava rock containing gas cavities which have been filled with secondary minerals.

Andesite. A fine-grained extrusive rock composed primarily of plagioclase and one or more of the dark-coloured ferromagnesian minerals (eg, biotite, hornblende, pyroxene).

Basalt. A general term for dark-coloured ferromagnesian igneous rocks, commonly extrusive but locally intrusive (eg, as dykes), composed chiefly of calcic plagioclase and clinopyroxene.

Cabochon. An unfaceted cut gemstone of domed or convex form. The top is smoothly polished; the back, or base, is usually flat and often unpolished. In outline it may be any shape.

Chalcedony. A hydrous cryptocrystalline variety of quartz. It is commonly microscopically fibrous, may be translucent or semitransparent, and has a nearly wax-like lustre. Colour may be white, greyish, pale blue, brown, or black. It has a lower density than ordinary quartz. Some agates have been investigated under the scanning electron microscope. The 'fibres' of chalcedony, visible under the polarizing microscope, are not real fibres (crystal individuals) but consist of subparticles whose texture is seen to be both granular and platy.

Chemical differentiation. As used here, the process by which dense homogeneous silica gels develop layers of different chemical and mineralogical composition.

Clear chalcedony layer. A relatively thin layer of clear or nearly clear chalcedony forming the outermost zone of most agates. It is the first layer in agate to crystallize (by spherulitic crystallization) during its formation. It thus encloses for a time the rest of the uncrystallized agate material (nascent agate).

Colloid. Any fine-grained material (silica particles, for example) in suspension.

Containment forces in agate. Many agates are affected by internal dynamic forces which cause distortion of the layers of nascent agate, producing such structures as tubes of escape and dilatations on the tubes of escape. If these forces are strong enough they will also produce rents in the clear chalcedony layer, and the consequent formation of agate dykes.

Crystallization. The process by which matter becomes crystalline, from a gaseous, fluid, or dispersed state.

Diffusion. As used here, diffusion is the process of movement of the chemical compounds of silica, water, and pigments through dense silica gels occupying gas cavities in lavas.

Dilatation on the tube of escape. A balloon-like swelling on the tube of escape (*qv*) situated near the clear chalcedony layer, to which it generally points. It often contains the same material as the centre of the agate.

Experimental mineralogy. A branch of mineralogy dealing with the laboratory study of reactions designed to elucidate mineral forming processes. The term includes experiments relating to the physical properties or physical chemistry of minerals,

mineral melts, or solutions coexisting with solid or non-solid mineral material.

Faceted gemstone. A natural gemstone on which polished plane surfaces (facets) have been developed by a lapidary.

Gemstone rough. An uncut gemstone.

Geode. A geode forms when a gas cavity in a lava is first lined with banded chalcedony and then filled incompletely towards its centre with inward projecting crystals which may be of quartz, calcite, or other minerals.

Grid. A network composed of two sets of uniformly spaced parallel lines, usually intersecting at right angles and forming squares, superimposed on a map to permit identification of ground locations by means of a system of co-ordinates – thus yielding a grid reference number.

Lapidary. Lapidary has two meanings: (a) a cutter, grinder, and polisher of coloured stones, such as agates; and (b) the art of cutting gems.

Meteoric water. Water derived mainly from the earth's atmosphere.

Nascent agate. A term used here to describe all compositional stages in the evolution of an agate-forming gel prior to its crystallization.

Old Red Sandstone. A thick sequence of non-marine, predominantly red sedimentary rocks, chiefly sandstones, conglomerates, and shales, representing the Devonian System in parts of Great Britain and elsewhere in NW Europe. The agate-bearing lavas of Scotland, some 380 million years old, occur within this sequence.

Quartz. Quartz, in its narrow definition, is anhydrous crystalline silica, a very common mineral composed of silicon dioxide. It may occur as distinct crystals. It is hard and durable and may on occasion form such gemstones as rock crystal, amethyst, citrine and smoky quartz (cairngorm).

Rent. The crack or fracture commonly seen in the clear chalcedony layer of agates where this layer is approached by a tube of escape with or without a dilatation. It is a late feature of agate formation.

Secondary mineral. A mineral formed later than the rock enclosing it, usually at the expense of an earlier-formed primary mineral (a mineral formed at the same time as the rock enclosing it), as a result of weathering, metamorphism, or solution.

Segregation. As used in this book, segregation means that a feature has formed as a result of the rearrangement of constituents within a dense silica gel after the gel's deposition in a gas cavity; pigments homogeneously distributed in a gel, for example, may be separated into coloured bands.

Silica gel. A silica gel is a siliceous substance in a colloidal state that allows diffusion of its constituents. No two gels in gas cavities are exactly the same in composition or behaviour and the agates formed from these gels are observed never to be exactly alike in structure, composition or colour.

Silicon carbide grits. These are loose powders of various grain size (grade) used in the grinding and lapping of gemstones. Silicon carbide is made by baking together clay and coke in an electric furnace. The powders or grits may also be compressed into wheels or bonded to paper or cloth.

Skin of agate. The greenish (or brownish) mineral matter found between the exterior of an agate and the walls of its cavity. One or more silicate minerals may make up this skin.

Spherulitic cystallization. In this context, spherulitic crystallization occurs in the clear chalcedony layer and is characterized by the dense growth of chalcedony fibres within hemispherical masses which themselves are intricately intermixed, although sometimes separated from each other (see figs 35 and 39). Crystallization in succeeding layers is characterized by long, parallel to subparallel, fibrous growths of chalcedony.

Tertiary. The first period of the Cenozoic era (after the Cretaceous of the Mesozoic era and before the Quaternary), thought to have covered the span of time between 65 and 3 to 2 million years ago. The Tertiary agate-bearing lavas mentioned in the text were formed about 50 million years ago.

Tube of escape. Agates sliced open commonly show chalcedonic bands pinched or squeezed into tube-like forms (tubes of escape) directed towards the clear chalcedony layer where they may swell into dilatations. They sometimes connect with a rent in the clear chalcedony layer, which in turn connects with an agate dyke. A tube of escape indicates that chalcedony or quartz in some agates has undergone deformation just before crystallization. This term and that of dilatation was first coined by M. F. Heddle in 1901.

Vesicle. In this context a cavity of any shape in a lava, formed by the entrapment of a gas bubble during the solidification of the lava.

Weathering. The destructive process by which rocks, on exposure to atmospheric agents at or near the earth's surface, are changed in colour, texture, composition or hardness.

Zeolite. A generic name for a large group of white, colourless, red or yellow, hydrous aluminosilicates that are analogous in composition to the feldspars, with sodium, calcium and potassium (rarely barium or strontium) as their chief metals. Zeolites have long been known to occur as well-formed crystals in cavities in basalt.

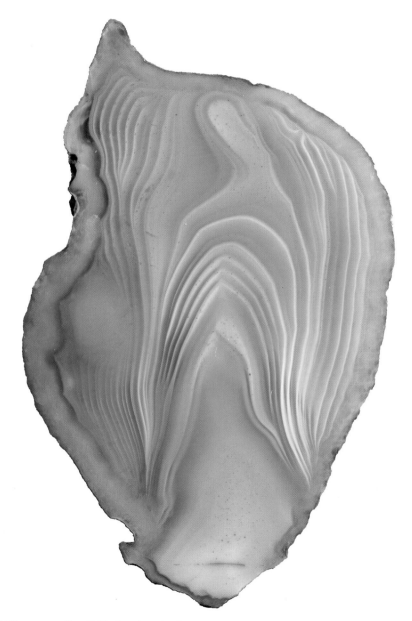

165 Flame agate from Ballindean (see also fig 72)

Bibliography

Anderson, J. (1901–2). Notice of cists discovered in a cairn at Cairnhill, Parish of Monaquhitter, Aberdeenshire and at Doune, Perthshire. *Proceedings of the Society of Antiquaries of Scotland* **36**: 675–88.

Bates, R. L. & Jackson, J. A. (1987). *Glossary of geology* (3rd edn). Alexandria, Virginia: American Geological Institute. This authoritative work has been used in compiling the glossary of this agate book.

Bauer, M. (1904). *Precious stones*. London: Charles Griffen.

Croucher, R. & Woolley, A. R. (1982). *Fossils, minerals and rocks, collection and preservation*. London: British Museum (Natural History); Cambridge University Press.

Dake, H. C., Fleener, F. L. & Wilson, B. H. (1938). *Quartz family minerals: a handbook for the mineral collector*. New York: McGraw Hill Book Co.

Edwards, D. H. (1921). *Among the fisher folk of Usan and Ferryden*. Brechin: Brechin Advertiser.

Ellis, C. (1954). *The pebbles on the beach*. London: Faber & Faber.

Frondel, C. (1962). *The system of mineralogy* vol. 3 (Silica Minerals). New York: John Wiley & Sons.

Frondel, C. (1985). Systematic compositional zoning in the quartz fibres of agates. *American Mineralogist* **70**: 975–9.

Greg, R. P. & Lettsom, W. G. (1858). *Manual of the mineralogy of Great Britain and Ireland*. London: John Van Voorst.

Heddle, M. F. (1901). *The mineralogy of Scotland* 1: 58–80 ('Agate'). Edinburgh: David Douglas.

Hughes, G. (1978). *A pictorial history of gems and jewellery*. Oxford: Phaidon.

Landmesser, M. (1984). Das Problem der Achatgenese. *Mitteilungen der Pollichia* Band 72, 5–137. Bad Dürkheim: Pollichia-Museum. A useful article in which theories of agate formation published since the middle of the nineteenth century are described and evaluated. In particular the theory, proposed in 1915 by R. E. Liesegang, which suggested that internal rhythmic precipitations of Fe-pigments spontaneously produce banded structures (Liesegang rings) in silica gels in rocks, is discredited. Some fundamentals of agate genesis are elaborated upon. An interesting series of scanning electron photographs of chalcedonic banding in spherulites is presented. These show that the 'fibres' of chalcedony, visible under the polarizing microscope, are not real fibres (crystal individuals) but consist of subparticles.

Landmesser, M. (1987). Das Rätsel Achat: Structuren, Probleme, Theorien. *Offizieller Katalog der 24 Mineralientage München '87 (Achat: Eiszeit: Siegerland)*, 65–88. One of eleven articles, by different authors, on agate, in a lavishly illustrated publication.

Lieper, H. Ed. (1966). *The agates of North America*. San Diego: Lapidary Journal.

Mawe, J. (1821). *Familiar lessons on mineralogy and geology* (3rd edn). London: Longman, Hurst et al.

Nassau, K. (1984). *Gemstone enhancement*. London: Butterworths.

Nimlin, J. (1974). *Let's look at Scottish gemstones*. Norwich: Jarrold & Sons.

Quick, L. (1963). *The book of agates*. Philadelphia: Chilton Books.

Rodgers, P. R. (1975). *Agate collecting in Britain*. London: B. T. Batsford Ltd.

Sinkankas, J. (1984). *Gem cutting: a lapidary's manual* (3rd edn.). New York: Van Nostrand Rheinhold Company.

Smith, J. (1910). *Semi-precious stones of Carrick*. Kilwinning: A. W. Cross.

Wheeley, H. (1976). *Take your pick to Agate Creek*. Melbourne: Gemcraft Publications Pty. Ltd. Richly illustrated.

Zodac, P. Ed. (1936). *Rocks and minerals*. Peekshill, New York. The September-October issue of this magazine has twenty-four articles on agates.

British Library CIP Data
Macpherson, H. G.
  Agates.
1. Agates
I. Title
553.8′7

Author: Dr H. G. Macpherson
Photographers: NMS Ian Larner, Doreen Moyes, R. J. Reekie, Ken Smith; BM (NH) Frank Greenaway
Aerial photographs: Patricia Macdonald
Diagrams and maps: Helen Jackson
Design: Publications Office of the National Museums of Scotland
Typesetting: Advanced Filmsetters (Glasgow) Ltd
Printing and binding: Times Offset Pte Ltd
Other picture sources:
  Figs 16 to 17 data copied and adapted from published maps of the British Geological Survey; fig 125 after Max Bauer (1904); fig 126 Tourist Office, Idar-Oberstein; fig 127 Richard S. Mitchell; fig 138 after John Mawe (1821); fig 139 Hunterian Museum; figs 140 to 142, 145, 146 and 149 British Museum (Natural History); figs 141, 143 and 144 by courtesy of the Board of Trustees of the Victoria and Albert Museum; figs 140 to 146 picture research by Sue Farley-Green, BM(NH).

We are grateful to Dr Roger Harding, BM(NH) for his help with BM(NH) specimens; Dr Alison Sheridan, NMS, for providing items for fig 123; and George Dalgleish, NMS, for items for figs 147 and 148.

Reprinted for HMSO, 1993.

ISBN 0 11 310012 4